P9-CUK-160

Journaling

Engagements in Reading, Writing, and Thinking

by Karen Bromley

New York • Toronto • London • Auckland • Sydney

excerpt from: Judith M. Newman, "Online: From Far Away,"
Language Arts, November 1989

No part of this publication may be reproduced in whole or in part,
or stored in a retrieval system, or transmitted in any form or by any
means, electronic or mechanical, photocopying, recording, or
otherwise, without written permission of the publisher. For information regarding permission, write to Scholastic Inc., 555 Broad-
way, New York, NY 10012.

ISBN 0–590–49478–3

Cover design by Vincent Ceci

Cover illustration by Vincent Ceci

Book design and interior illustration by
Ellen Matlach Hassell for
Boultinghouse and Boultinghouse, Inc.

Copyright © 1993 by Karen Bromley. All rights reserved.

Printed in the U.S.A.

**For C. and S.
who help with the paperclips**

Contents

Acknowledgments

The names of many teachers and students appear throughout this text. The teachers shared with me what worked and what didn't work as they used the journals described here, and the students allowed their journal entries to be reproduced. I am grateful to both, for their application of the theory and research that underlie journal writing and their stories, without which this book would not be possible.

The teachers I would like to thank include Kim Ames, Joylyn Bailey-Tyburczy, Sue Bertoni, Jane Bonner, Mary Jo Feroleito, Deborah Frank, Sue Guerin, Carol Hogan, Jan Jakubowicz, Nancy Mangialetti, Diane Mannix, Debbie Miller, Catherine Paniccia, Maryann Parker, Julie Pitts, Barbara Reardon, Sheila Salmon, Betsy Sarver, Kerri Schlimmer, Kisten Schroeder, Rebecca Slater, Pat Turner-Massey, Gregg Veatch, Sandy Whitehouse, Mark Williams, Julie Wilson, Debbie Winters and Kara Zajac. Jennifer Boushie deserves special thanks for her help with the annotated bibliography in Appendix A.

I would also like to thank Terry Cooper and Joan Novelli, editors at Scholastic Professional Books, for their thoughtful questions and helpful suggestions.

Introduction

Many years ago, as a third grade teacher, my students and I created a journal that Rudyard Kipling, famous for the How and Why tales we were reading, might have kept. A few years later, as a K–6 reading teacher, I worked with 5th and 6th grade teachers to improve their students' comprehension by writing predictions about new stories in their personal journals. As a university professor for the past 15 years, I have had students keep: logs and personal journals in which they reflect on their teaching, response journals in which they react to literature, buddy journals in which they share ideas and information with peers, and double entry journals where they learn to make associations and rethink their ideas. I teach courses and give inservice workshops on the writing process. I see and work closely with classroom teachers and students who are involved in all sorts of journal writing. I know how important the connection is between journals and the writing process and I use both in my own writing.

This book grows out of these various experiences with journals and writing. It is meant to give teachers who are new to journal writing a place to start, and teachers who have used or are using journals some fresh ideas.

The chapters that follow present 13 different types of journals. Through the stories of 25 classroom teachers (pre-K to high school) and examples of their students' journal writing, you'll discover ways to build a more effective journal writing program in your own classroom. You'll find the how-to's for each type of journal, discussions of problems teachers and students sometimes encounter, and suggested solutions for those problems.

Nearly every chapter links children's literature with journal writing. That's because children's books serve as an inspiration for journal writing, as models of writing and even as models of journal writing. An annotated bibliography of more than 50 books for K–12 in which main characters keep journals or the writing is in journal format is included (see Appendix A).

Finally, while all of the journals are designed to develop the literacy of all students, you'll find special sections devoted to using journals to help ESL students learn English, to build the writing fluency of students who have learning problems, to promote cooperation among students, to encourage collaboration between and among teachers, and to strengthen home-school connections.

Writing this book has been fun and thought provoking. It has helped me see how critical the connections are between reading, writing, and thinking, and how important journals can be for literacy and learning. I hope it's enjoyable and easy for you to read and that it inspires and informs the journal writing you and your students do!

—KB

CHAPTER 1

Why Use Journals?

Journal, Learning Log, Day Book, Free Writing, Draw-and-Tell, Friday Writing, Dialogue Journal, Buddy Journal, Double Entry Journal, Writer's Notebook, Team Journal, Electronic Dialogue Journal, Kid Watching Journal, Go-Home Journal, Traveling. . .

No matter what the special name, a journal is usually a bound volume, notebook, or booklet in which students write freely, usually for themselves, perhaps for later rereading, but often for others to read and respond to as well. A journal might also be a collection of electronic correspondence between students who communicate via a computer and modem.

How does writing in journals also contribute to your students' reading and thinking? Writing invites and engages writers to read as well as think. Journals provide students with records of their own thoughts, ideas, and observations, and so invite them to reread, revisit, and perhaps revise past thoughts.

Applebee (1984) says that the permanence of print, the explicitness required in writing, and the active nature of writing, provide a medium for exploring our own reasoning abilities. We know that writing is more than the expression of a predetermined message. In the process of putting thoughts and ideas down on paper, writers often create new knowledge and develop awareness of new ideas, concepts, and relationships that they did not previously know.

Writing in journals can cause "the light in the attic" to go on for your students, allowing them to think and process information more precisely and in ways that are different from spoken language production. Journal writing engages your students in both the expression and creation of thought. Indeed, there is a close reading-writing-thinking relationship.

Using Journals in Your Classroom

You can use journals with your students in a variety of ways to build reading-writing-thinking relationships. For example, if you teach young children, you can encourage them to draw pictures in their journals and talk about them, since drawing and talking are natural precursors to writing. Young children generally talk easily about their drawings and you can record what they say about their pictures on corresponding pages of their journals.

If you teach older students, you can encourage them to explore their thoughts, ideas, and opinions on a variety of personally chosen topics and record these in journals. Older students often choose to write responses to literature or summarize and synthesize learning in science or social studies in their journals. Entries like these can become the basis for small group and class conversations and discussions in which your students share and extend their understandings and learning.

For both young children and older students, it's important to encourage invented spelling in their journal writing and focus on the content of the message, rather than on form or mechanics of writing. When your students are able to express themselves and write freely in their journals without fear of grades or evaluation, journals become a place where they can experiment with language and thinking, where knowledge can unfold and grow, and where they can learn to communicate effectively with themselves and with others.

As you read entries and write replies, you'll encourage the reading-writing-thinking relationship. Some tips to guide your responses include:

1. Support the message. Connect with what your students say in some way, whether by acknowledging, praising, agreeing, or sharing your own similar ideas.

2. Provide information. This is important especially when an entry indicates that a student misunderstands, does not understand, or just lacks facts.

3. Clarify and extend thinking. When an entry is unclear, ask for clarification. Challenge students to rethink, reflect, and stretch their minds.

Reading your students' journal entries also gives you a window on their thinking and literacy development. Consider keeping your own journal in which you record annecdotes and observations about the progress of particular students. In many cases, when you note behavior and performance, you will see patterns emerging that you might not necessarily notice without such a record to look back on, examine, and interpret. Journal entries can help you document students' strengths and needs, and plan for the kind of instruction that will be most helpful.

As well as establishing opportunities that build the reading-writing-thinking relationship for your students, journals can help accomplish a variety of other goals in your curriculum, including:

• giving you a clearer idea of your students' strengths, needs, interests, attitudes, and understandings;

- encouraging fluency in handwriting as your students practice using written language in a safe and risk-free environment;
- helping non-English speakers learn English by writing to English language users and reading their entries;
- improving syntax, vocabulary, and standard spelling for students who have writing difficulties as well as for students learning English;
- promoting cooperative learning as students working in pairs and small groups read and write in each other's journals;
- establishing friendships for students with special needs through peer interactions in journals;
- providing important links with parents as journals travel back and forth between school and your students' homes.

Journals are indeed versatile tools for learning. According to Macrorie (1987), "the payoffs from using journals in classrooms are. . . astounding" (p.ii). In the remaining chapters of this handbook you will learn how to implement a variety of journals and discover the payoffs they provide as you and your students grow as readers, writers, and thinkers.

References

Applebee, A. (1984). Writing and reasoning. *Review of Educational Research, 54* (4), 577–596.

Macrorie, K. (1987). Forward. In *The Journal Book,* Ed. by T. Fulwiler. Portsmouth, NH: Heinemann.

CHAPTER 2

Journal Writing in Children's Books

September 5, 1839
I will always remember my first sight of White Island
where we lived after my family and I left the mainland. . .
The year was 1839 and it was sunset when we were set
ashore on that lonely rock where the lighthouse looked
down on us like some tall, black-capped giant.

This is the first entry in a journal written by a young girl about her experiences growing up on an island off the coast of New England where her father was the lighthouse keeper. The original journal, written by Celia Thaxter, has been adapted and illustrated by Loretta Krupinski in *Celia's Island Journal* (Little, Brown, 1992). Krupinski's lovely realistic paintings of the sea life, birds and flowers that lived on the island at that time make this journal picture book a special blend of storytelling and nature observation for you and your students.

May 14
 Every year on this date, the cows get put out to pasture. When I ask why this date, everybody has a different answer.

 Fred, the hired man, says that the grass isn't ready till now.
 Father says that the cows' stomachs aren't ready for green grass before today.
 Mother says they're both wrong. She says it's just the way it's always been and nobody's ever asked why.
 I think she's right. She usually is.

This is an example of the monthly diary entries written by a 12 year-old boy in which he documents his life in the 1800's on a farm in new England. Full-page color illustations in *Farm Boy's Year* by David McPhail (Atheneum, 1992), accompany each entry showing your students a life that combines hard work and play.

These two excerpts are from recently published historical fiction picture books in which main characters keep journals. Journal writing appears in other genres of children's literature as well, including realistic fiction, fantasy, biography, and nonfiction. In some of the 50 titles included in Appendix A, the main characters keep journals. In others, the books themselves are written in journal format. How can you use published journals in your classroom?

Following are several ways you can use this special group of books in your classroom.

1. To introduce journal writing:

Use published journals to introduce journal writing—the main characters are excellent role models for your students! Share excerpts from an amusing book such as *Henry Reed, Inc.*, by K. Robertson (Penguin, 1989), or a serious book like *The Year Without Michael*, by S. Pfeffer (Bantam, 1988), or *Robyn's Book: A True Diary* by Robyn Miller (Scholastic, 1986). Make these and other titles available in your classroom library so students can read them independently.

2. To motivate writing:

Share these books as a way to inject interest if motivation in journal writing wanes. Each day before journal writing, read a few entries from a published journal. Hearing what a main character or author wrote in a journal will have a powerful effect on your students and encourage their writing. Seeing personal journals that were not intended for publication but have been published, may give your students incentive to write their own. Two examples of this are *The Diary of Nina Kosterina* by M. Ginsburg (Crown, 1968) and *Letters From Rifka* by K. Hesse (Holt, 1992).

3. To model different kinds of writing:

Present these books as models of different types of journals to imitate. For example, read excerpts from a travel journal to students before they go on a vacation and encourage them to document their trips in their own travel journals. Read a science journal like *An Owl In the House*, by B. Heinrich (Little, Brown, 1990), to your students and then have them keep one. Or, read a humorous journal like Paul Zindel's *Amazing and Death Defying Diary of Eugene Dingman* (HarperCollins, 1987) and encourage students to try humorous writing.

4. To connect your curriculum:

Integrate the reading of published journals and journal writing with your curriculum. For example, you might coordinate the type of journal reading and writing your students do with science or social studies units. If your class will be studying Westward Expansion, read journals like *Joshua's Westward Journal* by J. Anderson (Morrow, 1987) or *Cassie's Journey: Going West in the 1860's* by Brett Harvey (Holiday House, 1992) and have your students keep similar journals.

5. To break through writer's block:

Share these books with students who suffer from writer's block. An awareness of all the different kinds of journals that have been written often helps students see possibilities for keeping their own journals. For example, in *Nobody Is Perfick.* by Bernard Waber (Houghton Mifflin, 1970), a young girl keeps lists of "Ten-Best" in her journal (days of the year, friends of the year, colors, things to do, television programs, games, songs, books, ice cream flavors, things I want to be when I grow up, ways to fall asleep on a hot night). A student with writer's block can surely get an idea for beginning to write from this funny book.

The remainder of this chapter takes a closer look at using these books in your journal writing program. Full annotations for the children's books mentioned here and in other chapters, appear in Appendix A.

Present Day Journals

Day 1
   Louie laid his hot dog down for two minutes while he went through his entire suitcase looking for issue #14 of Samurai Surfer. . . Louie turned around and his hot dog was gone. Not just plain gone or dropped down a crack behind the bunk, but disappeared!

This is the first entry in *Petey Moroni's Camp Runamok Diary,* by Pat Cummings (Bradbury, 1992). In this humorous journal, a young black boy keeps track of all the food that disappears each day for 2 weeks at camp because a raccoon is on the loose. Full-color illustrations include multi-racial campers and one in a wheelchair.

Many other journal books are set in the present and with humor depict the feelings, emotions, thoughts, and problems of growing up today. In Beverly Cleary's *Strider* (Morrow, 1991) and *Dear Mr. Henshaw* (Morrow, 1984), 11 year-old Leigh Botts writes about how he makes friends at a new

school in California and grows to accept his parents' separation and divorce.

In *The Diary of Latoya Hunter* by Latoya Hunter (Crown, 1992), a 12 year-old black girl describes conflicts with her mother, growing up in the Bronx, and, as shared here, her first year (and day) of junior high school:

It is hard to believe that this is the day I have anticipated and looked forward to for such a long time. The sun still rose in the East and set in the West, the crisis in Iraq is still going strong, and Oprah Winfrey still preached at 4:00 about other people's business. This may sound funny but somewhere in the back of my mind I thought the world would stop for my first day of junior high. The day proved me wrong, and I've grown to realize that nothing will be quite as I dreamed it up.

In other books for older readers, journal writing has a powerful effect on female main characters. In *Me and My Mona Lisa Smile,* by S. Hayes (Lodestar, 1981), journal writing and an English teacher help a girl gain confidence in herself through her writing abilities. In *The Last of Eden*, by S. Tolan (Scribner, 1981), Michelle loves writing so much that she takes her journal with her everywhere.

Fantasy Journals

Graham Oakley's *The Diary of a Churchmouse* (Atheneum, 1987) is an example of humorous fantasy in a journal that relates a year in the life of the church mice in an English church vestry. Humphrey keeps the journal in which he tells with dry humor and comic detail about the lives of his friend Arthur, Sampson the cat, and the other church mice. In this entry, Humphrey's ego shows:

1st April
Everybody's telling everybody else that there's a cat behind them or that there's a knot in their tails or some such non-sense. I've no time for it myself. . . I had a message to rush across to the rectory and take a phone call. They'd hung up by the time I got there. I waited all day but they forgot to call back. . . After all, royalty's much too busy opening dog shows and parliaments and things to remember everything.

Carefully detailed color pictures accompany the entries and tell a humorous story, different from the text.

Journals From the Past

Celia and the young farm boy mentioned at the beginning of this chapter, as well as main characters in other books, tell stories in their journals that help young students experience the past. For example Jenny, a present day eleven year-old, learns about the world just before World War II when she discovers her aunt's diary in the book *A Certain Magic* by Doris Orgel (Dial, 1976). Excerpts from the diary are part of this suspenseful story. Laura Ingalls Wilder's stories, *The First Four Years* (HarperCollins, 1986) and *On the Way Home* (HarperCollins, 1962) help children become part of the hardships and happiness of a family that lives on the prairie frontier of early America.

There are several good books written as journals that allow older students to experience the past vicariously. For example, they can learn what it was like to live in New England in the 1800's from Catherine, the girl who writes the entries in *A Gathering of Days* by Joan Blos (Scribner, 1979). They can experience winter on a ranch in Wyoming in the early 1900's as they live with the main character in *Bunkhouse Journal* by D.J. Hamm (Scribner, 1990). With *The Diary of Trilby Frost* by D. Glasser (Holiday House, 1976), they can put themselves in the place of a teenage girl who is growing up in rural Tennessee in the early 1900's and must deal with the death of her father and best friend.

They can learn about the values, conflicts, and experiences of a young soldier in Vietnam in *A GI's Vietnam Diary: 1968–1969* by Daniel Yezzo (Franklin Watts, 1964). Or, in *The Diary of Nina Kosterina* by M. Ginsburg (Crown, 1968), share Nina's experiences with the horrors of growing up in Germany and Russia, two countries torn by World War II.

Travel Journals

Several picture books in journal format document travel and the deeper understandings main characters acquire as a result.

Nettie, a young girl who travels from New York to Virginia just before the Civil War, writes to her friend in *Nettie's Trip South* by A. Turner (Macmillan, 1987):

Addie, I can't get this out of my thoughts: If we slipped into a black skin like a tight coat, everything would change.

This powerful account of Nettie's reaction to slavery is based on the real diary of the author's great grandmother and is accompanied by soft black and white pencil sketches.

This excerpt is from *Cassie's Journey: Going West in the 1860's* by Brett Harvey (Holiday House, 1992):

We're on our way to California! I'm riding up high with Papa, and the wind is rocking the wagon. When I look back I can see a long line of wagons curling behind us like a snake in the dust.

In this book a young girl relates the hardships and dangers of traveling with her family in a covered wagon from Missouri to California. It is based on actual diaries kept by women during their westward travels. Soft pencil drawings add a warm, interesting glimpse of the past.

A book for younger readers with a male main character who travels with his family through the prairie in the mid 1800's is *Joshua's Westward Journal* by J. Anderson (Morrow, 1987). For older readers, Kathryn Lasky's *Beyond the Divide* (Morrow, 1986) documents a 14 year-old Amish girl's travel west with her father in search of an accepting community in which to settle.

Pedro's Journal, by Pam Conrad (Caroline House, 1991) begins with:

August 3
The ship's roster of the Santa Maria has me down as Pedro de Salcedo, ship's boy. And the captain of this ship. . . has hired me not for my great love of the sea, nor for my seamanship, but because I have been taught to read and write, and

he thinks it will be useful to have me along.

This is the diary of young Pedro Salcedo who is a Spanish ship's boy aboard the Santa Maria. His journal entries and pencil sketches tell the story of Christopher Columbus and give your students a firsthand account of one of the most famous voyages ever.

In another picture book travel journal, *The Log of Christopher Columbus* by S. Lowe (Philomel, 1992), students can read adaptations of excerpts from Columbus' diary. In it he reveals his fears, disappointments, and excitement about his first voyage.

Biography Based on Journals

There are some biographies for older students that are based on journals people kept. These books may motivate your students to write about their own special experiences.

Two deal with people who had special needs. In *Flowers For Algernon*, by D. Keyes (Bantam, 1970), a 33 year-old retarded bakery worker relates his experiences with teachers, doctors, and scientists in modifying his intelligence. In *Robyn's Book: A True Diary,* by Robyn Miller (Scholastic, 1986), a young woman describes her life with cystic fibrosis. An excerpt follows:

For the first sixteen years of my life I enjoyed something few kids like me experience—good health. I always knew I was sick, knew my disease was progressive, even knew it was fatal. But the implications seldom hit home or made me worry.

One well known biography that is based on a journal the author kept herself is *The Diary of a Young Girl* by Anne Frank (Washington Square Press, 1987). It is also available in a large print edition (Cornerstone, 1987) for students with visual impairments.

Several biographies for older students relate the lives of successful writers and may motivate your students who aspire to become writers themselves:

Chapters: My Growth As A Writer by Lois Duncan (Little, Brown, 1949)

Invincible Louisa by C. Meigs (about Louisa May Alcott's life) (Little, Brown, 1933)

My Diary-My World by E. Yates (Westminster Press, 1981)

My Widening World: The Continuing Diary of Elizabeth Yates by E. Yates (Westminster Press, 1983)

Journals in Science

Two examples of journals kept by naturalists, *A Snake Lover's Diary* by B. Brenner (HarperCollins, 1970), and *An Owl In the House: A Naturalist's Diary*, by B. Heinrich (Little, Brown, 1990) provide good models for science writing. In the first, a young boy keeps a diary with photos of the physical characteristics and habitats of snakes he catches. In the second, called a field journal, the author's notes, drawings, and photos follow the development of a great horned owlet from captivity to independence in the wild. When they keep journals similar to these, your students can sharpen their powers of observation and descriptive writing.

To Learn More

To get started with journals, from writing to editing and publishing, you might find the following books helpful:

The Young Writer's Handbook by Stephen and Susan Tchudi (Aladdin, 1984)

Writing Down the Days: 365 Creative Journaling Ideas for Young People by L. M. Dahlstrom (Free Spirit Press, 1990)

325 Creative Prompts for Personal Journals by J.A. Senn (Scholastic, 1992)

How To Make Your Own Books by H. Weiss (HarperCollins, 1974)

CHAPTER 3

Personal Journal

If we endeavored more to improve ourselves by reflection, by making a business of thinking, and giving our thoughts form and expression, we should be led to read not to contradict and confute, nor to believe and take for granted, but to weigh and consider. *Henry David Thoreau* (Muller, 1988, p. 365)

Henry David Thoreau, a social and political activist and naturalist, began a real personal journal when he was 18. From this journal came his two most famous books, *Walden* and *A Week On the Concord and Merrimack Rivers*. Thoreau believed that journaling made a more thoughtful person.

Like Thoreau's, personal journals or private diaries are usually first-person records of day-to-day incidents of life, feelings and emotions, ideas, and reflections. In personal journals, students can work through dilemmas, give voice to inner thoughts and feelings, discuss adventures and dreams, and become fluent, comfortable writers. Personal journals give students opportunities to find and exercise their own distinctive and indivdiual voices.

Typically, for the adult writer, the personal journal is written only for the writer's eyes and is not read by anyone else. But in the classroom setting, you may want to read your students' journals and occasionally ask them to read entries to the class. Asking students to share entries orally validates the keeping of these journals, as well as allows students a way to get to know one another better. Hearing (or reading) students' entries will also give you insights into their world and their literacy development.

Published Personal Journals

While some personal journals are written for the writer's eyes only and are not read by anyone else, many personal journals are read by others and become published. These journals are inspiring ways for you and your students to know about real people, including the things they have done and the conflicts they have felt.

To introduce your students to personal journals, you might want to read excerpts from published personal journals, such as Thoreau's. (With younger students, you might share a fictional picture book example of personal journals, such as *The Diary of a Church Mouse* or *Farm Boy's Year*, both described in Chapter 2.)

To inspire students' own journal writing ideas, talk about the thoughts and conflicts of the journal authors you read. For example, *My Diary My World* (Westminster, 1981), Elizabeth Yates' autobiography in journal form, shows the struggles of a young girl growing up in a family that does not support her dreams of being a writer. She writes:

> *I have a place of my own! A new garage has been built, and the top of it is to be a pigeon loft someday, but Father said I could use it for the time being. . . There's a window that looks across the fields to the pinewoods.*
>
> *I sit in the middle of the floor, looking out, and I think; then, when I'm ready to write, I turn around . . . Often it seems that writing is mostly thinking. . .*

Yates, your students might be interested to know, is the author of *Amos Fortune, Free Man* and more than 25 other books!

A G.I.'s Vietman Diary 1968–1969 by Dominick Yezzo (Franklin Watts, 1974) and *The Diary of Nina Kosterina*, translated by Mirra Ginsburg (Crown, 1968), are two more examples of published journals that you might use to introduce personal journal writing to your students. The first presents a day-to-day account of a young soldier's experiences in Vietnam—his thoughts, emotions, doubts, and insecurities as he fights a war he is unsure about. In the second, Nina writes movingly about her life from age 15 to 21 in Soviet Russia during Stalin's rule. Entries engage older readers personally in the great purges, trials, and terror that characterized the early days of World War II.

As well, your students might be particularly interested in published personal journals kept by people who never wrote in their diaries with this intention in mind. Ann Turner was inspired to write *Nettie's Trip South* (Macmillan, 1987) when she read a diary her great-grandmother kept on a trip from Albany, New York to Richmond, Virginia in 1859. In letters to her friend Addie, Nettie expresses her reactions to the horrors of the slavery she witnessed. From her diary, it is easy to see how these experiences helped Turner's great-gandmother become a staunch abolitionist in her later years. One entry follows:

> *There was a platform. There was a fat man in a tight white suit. There was a black woman on the platform. "Jump, aunt, jump!" the man shouted. Someone called out a price and she was gone. Gone, Addie, like a sack of flour pushed across a store counter.*

Publication of the personal logs Columbus kept on his trips to the new world has changed our view of Columbus as "discoverer," to one of "invader" and even "despoiler" (Konig, 1976). In Columbus' logs he tells about how he required every man and woman, and boy or girl of fourteen or older, in the province of Cibao on Hispaniola, to collect gold for the Spaniards. His log entries describe the cruel slaughter of the Arawak Indians when they did not present him with the gold he ordered them to bring him every three months. His journal also documents their mass suicides by cassava poison.

Karen's Journal

What is the form and what are the mechanics of the personal journal? If you are going to use this type of journal with your students, you will either want to have them purchase spiral notebooks or create their own journals. (Directions for making journals appear in Appendix B). You will also want to set aside a special time for journal writing. You may decide to do this in conjunction with independent reading time. In this way, what students read may influence what and how they write. Or, you may ask your students to write in their journals first thing in the morning, during the last few minutes of every day, or at some other convenient time.

Included here are selected entries from one student's personal journals written when she was in first and second grade. In one of Karen's first journal entries (Figure 3.1) she writes a list of her spelling words and draws pictures to accompany each. Karen's October journal entry (Figure 3.2) contains accu-

3.1 Karen drew pictures and wrote her spelling words in this entry in her first grade personal journal.

3.2 Karen copied this entry from a class-dictated story.

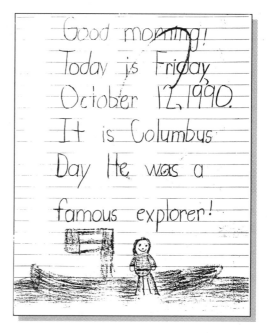

3.3 Karen used invented spelling and wrote about three distinctly different things.

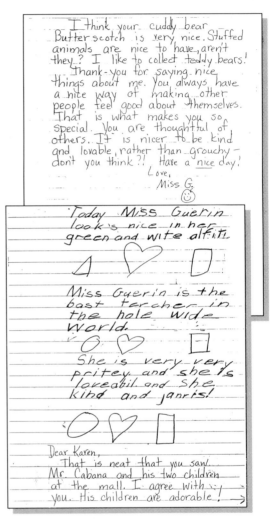

3.4 Karen's teacher writes a response to one of Karen's entries.

rate spelling for difficult words which she may have copied from the story the class dictated that morning. In her April entry (Figure 3.3), Karen feels confident enough to begin to use invented spelling and has moved away from copying a model. She seems to have a beginning concept of paragraphs and attends to punctuation, using quotation marks at the ends of each sentence. Although Karen begins her first grade journal with words and pictures, by November of her second grade year it is clear that she feels quite confident about writing on topics of her own choice (Figure 3.5).

Without the threat of evaluation or grades hanging over their heads, children often feel a release to write about their own real and immediate concerns. Clearly, Karen's dis-

taste for "sentencedicktashin" (Figure 3.5), an upcoming spelling test (Figure 3.6), writing 37 sentences in her journal (Figure 3.7), and the series of unfortunate happenings she describes (Figure 3.8) suggest that her journal is a place for personal feelings.

Looking at students' personal journals over an extended period of time can also

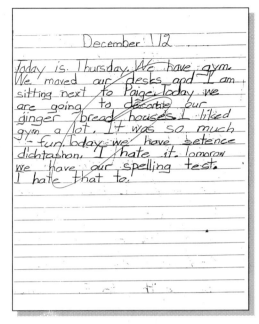

W.OW!

November 7

Today is Thursday. We have gym.
Today is a halfday. Lindsay is
comeing to my house after school.
I like having halfday's a lot.
Today is setencedicktashin.
I hate setencedichtashin. It is
not a lot of fun doing
setencedicktashin. I am going
to skateland today. I like to
skate.

3.5 *Evidence of invented spelling and an aversion for sentence dictation appear in an entry from Karen's second grade journal.*

3.6 *The teacher added a "G" for good and to indicate she had read Karen's entry.*

give you insight into their literacy development. Three of Karen's journal entries from April, May, and June (Figures 3.9–3.11), compared with previous entries (Figures 3.1–3.4), show her progress in writing. Over a two-year period, Karen's vocabulary and expressive language grew. Karen began by drawing pictures, writing single words, and copying sentences, and moved to using invented spelling and longer sentences to write about a variety of topics. In the later entries, Karen gives a hint of her sense of humor with an "April Fool" (Figure 3.9). She shows enthusiasm for school and life in general when she writes "I can not wait" several times (Figures 3.9–3.11). She also indicates how much she enjoys writing in her "jurnil" (Figure 3.10).

January 5

Today is Wednesday. We have
library and music. Today Paige
moved. I am sitting next
to no one. On Friday we get
our reeportcards. This Friday
Yours is Great!
is my birthday. Rose Anne
broat in her tambareen.
The 100th day is coming up. I
like doing my jurnil alot. It shows!
Yesterday I wrote 37 sentices
in my jurnil.
It was alot of fun for me.

3.7 *The teacher added brief sentences, showing Karen that she had read the entry.*

> February 12.
> Today is Wednesday. We have music
> and library. Today I forgot my
> lunch. And my cat made a mess
> out of the celer. And my
> brother pucched me. Today I
> get a sticker. On Friday we
> are going to go skiing. Tonight
> I am going skiing with my
> mothie and brother. Next
> week I am singing on the
> radeo with my brownie troop.
> wow.

3.8 Karen wrote in her journal about all the unfortunate things that happened to her that day.

> April 1.
> Today is Wednesday. We have
> library and music. I forgot
> my library books. Today is
> April Fools day. Today we
> are going to have
> a pizza party. I can
> not wait. For soda I
> brought diet coke. Today
> Shamboo pat a snake
> on my chair. Today we
> are doing more test. I
> think I did good on
> the test we did yesterday.
> Yesterday I got a book
> (over)

3.9 Karen shows her ability to document a wide variety of happenings in and out of school.

Variations on Entries

As well as being a place for your students to document their lives, personal journals are also a place for them to experiment with writing. Some students mix diary entries with stories or poems. Some students use the structure and form of familiar stories, or stories read aloud to them, as models to imitate. Students may borrow settings or characters from stories they hear or are reading and improvise on them in their personal journals. Or, students can use their journals to create original stories. So, merging personal journal writing time with independent reading time makes sense. In this way, you integrate reading and writing for your students and you allow the literature your students read to influence and find its way into their personal journals.

Journal Sharing

Often, teachers ask students to choose one entry per week to read to the class. This is usually a popular time—students generally enjoy sharing their writing and hearing each other's entries. It's important to remind students to read their entries just the way they were written. Without this stipulation, some students do not attempt to write meaningful entries and sharing can become an invitation to take part in ad-libbing and storytelling. Reading the words and language that are written helps preserve the integrity of the written word and encourages

> May 27
>
> Today is Wednesday. We have library and music. I love to write to our pen pals. It is getting close to my kittens birthday. Today for snack I have a browny. I can not wait until the day of the play. I hope I can write twelve sentences in my jurnil so I do not have to get any seet work. Today is the 161 day of school. It is getting very close to the end of the year. For the science fair we made a few flowers that will videbonate into the flower and that will make the flower turn in to a surtan color. I love to write in my jurnil. Today in the library we are not going to get books out, but we are going to watch movies and read books. Today we have Junor Great Books.

3.10 Karen's spelling and grammar improved over the course of the year.

> June 4
>
> Today is Thursday. We have gym. Today is the day of our play. I feel nervis. My Mother and father are coming to the play. On Monday our pen pals came. It was alot of fun. I am excited about the play. I am the Wicked Wich of the West. Yesterday a girl named Lori came to our class room and she talked about animals because she worked at an Animal Hospital. That is were my kitten goes. I can not wait until our play. I hope I do not mess up! I hope the parents like our play alot. I like all off the costumes.

3.11 In the journal, Karen recognized her own feelings of nervousness about the play she will be in soon when her parents will be in the audience.

a sense of ownership of what students write.

Of course, when students are just learning the language or having difficulty with writing, you'll want to support them as they make verbal additions to what they have drawn or written and encourage the communication of meaning during oral sharing. And in the case of shy or hesitant students, you might ask them to choose entries for you to read. Before long, most will want to read their own entries.

As students continue to read selected entries over time, you'll see the benefits in more interesting content, clearer descriptions, fuller explanations, and improved form. When students share orally, they become more aware of what they have written and how it sounds. The response and encouragement they get from their audience is an important factor, too.

Tips For Success

1. What should you do about sensitive issues in entries? Some teachers find that writing in personal journals about individually chosen topics is a potential problem, since occasionally students reveal private and sensitive issues which put the teacher in an uncomfortable position. You may not know quite how to respond to some personal problems students reveal and you may wonder about your responsibility to notify authorities about certain situations.

A student may, for example, reveal neglect or physical abuse by a parent in a journal entry. In this case, talk to your principal about school policy and your legal responsibilities. You may also want to invite your school's guidance counselor or psychologist to join your class for personal journal writing and sharing so that you have an expert available in such cases.

2. How important is teacher response in the personal journal? For beginning writers and students who need a nudge to write in their journals, it is very important. As you can see from the checks, stars, and written responses of Karen's teachers, they did read her entries and often reacted to what she wrote.

Once a week, Karen's first grade teacher usually wrote an entry in the form of a letter (Figure 3.4 for an example), and this probably had an impact on what and how much Karen wrote. Certainly, her teacher's comments reinforced certain behaviors and affected how Karen felt about herself. Knowing that her entries would be read by someone and that what she said was important enough to receive a response, undoubtedly gave added impetus to Karen's writing.

3. Posing thoughtful questions that require more than "yes" or "no" answers can nudge your students to be more reflective and can trigger richer written responses from them. For example, Karen's teachers might have asked: "Can you describe what 'nervous' feels like?"

Karen's teacher, in turn, might share how she feels when she is nervous in order to help Karen discover that everyone gets nervous and that being nervous is normal and natural.

4. What systems for monitoring personal journals do teachers use? Some teachers merely check to see that students are writing something and do not read entries. Other teachers collect journals, read them, and check them off in some way, perhaps with checks and stars or by writing a response (Figures 3.1–3.2, 3.5–3.6, 3.8–3.10, and 3.4), as Karen's teachers did.

References

Konig, H. (1976). *Columbus: His Enterprises.* New York: Monthly Review Press.

Muller, G.H. (1988). (Ed.) *The McGraw-Hill Reader, 3rd Ed.* New York: McGraw-Hill.

Literature Response Journal

. . .a sourcebook, a repository for wanderings and wonderings, speculations, questionings. . . a place to explore thoughts, discover reactions, let the mind ramble—in effect, a place to make room for the unexpected
(p. 5, Flitterman-King, 1988)

. . .a treasure chest filled with spontaneous thoughts and ideas that otherwise would have been forgotten
(p. 41, Hancock, 1992)

These two descriptions of literature response journals give you a glimpse into the many reasons for using them in your classroom. Much has been written about this kind of journal, perhaps because it used with such success by so many teachers from elementary to college level.

Response to literature grows from interactions with print and is highly personal. The transactions, ideas, feelings, and associations one person has with print are often quite different than another person's. Each of us brings our own special background of experiences and prior knowledge to what is read and so each of us takes very different things away from that print. We each have

potentially different literary transactions with a story or poem (Rosenblatt, 1985).

When readers have efferent responses, they acquire information and ideas. When readers have aesthetic responses, they feel and experience what they read, having emotional responses as they "live through" what print describes. Of course, the responses readers have are affected by many things. For example, after reading *A Taste of Blackberries* by D. Smith (Crowell, 1973) in which a young boy deals with the bee sting death of a friend, students may clearly have aesthetic responses, while efferent responses may not be so obvious. With another type of book, for example a social studies text or non-fiction information book, students' responses may tend to be more efferent with little aesthetic or emotional response. Rosenblatt tells us that students' aesthetic responses are basic and necessary for efferent responses.

Literature response journals encourage these responses. In literature response journals, students interact on a personal level with stories and authors. For example, the response of the child who read *Princess Furball*, by Charlotte Huck (Scholastic, 1989) (Figure 4.1) shows that the student recognized Furball's patience and admired her actions as well. If your students trust you and feel safe within the pages of the journal, often what they write is deeper and more intense than what they might share in discussions or in graded papers. By providing encouraging, supportive comments to students' entries without evaluation, you can foster this atmosphere for journal writing. What your students have to say is the focus. You do not correct grammar or spelling and you do not give grades.

Letters to Teachers

Many teachers report success when students write entries in the form of letters to them. They encourage children to share honest reactions and do not grade entries. Many teachers write back to students, sharing their own responses and dialoguing about literature they, a group, or the class is reading. Teachers who use literature response journals say they learn much about students from them, for example:

- knowledge, understandings, uncertainties, and questions students have;

3/27

I liiKed the part when Princess Furball hid in the tree. And when she wore all those dresses at the balls. She was smart and patent. She lived hapily ever after. I loved the picthurs becaus they showed more about the story.

4.1 A second grader's response to a folktale.

- likes, dislikes, and preferences;
- feelings stories elicit;
- associations with previous experiences;
- connections with other books or authors;
- prediction and validation abilities;
- literary analysis skills (plot, characters, setting. . .);
- awareness and appreciation of author's style;
- identification of theme;
- application of theme to the larger world;
- approaches to reading and print;
- processes used for learning.

Literature response journals give your students opportunities to reflect on what

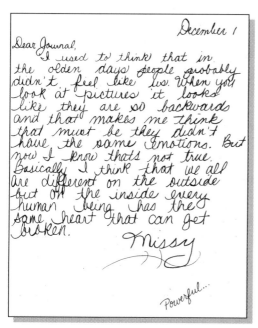

December 1

Dear Journal,
I used to think that in the olden days people probably didn't feel like us. When you look at pictures it looks like they are so backwards and that makes me think that must be they didn't have the same emotions. But now I know that's not true. Basically I think that we all are different on the outside but on the inside every human being has the same heart that can get broken.

Missy

Powerful...

4.2 *A sixth grader's entry in her literature response journal.*

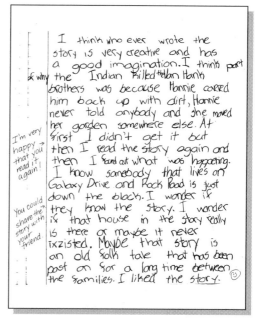

I think who ever wrote the story is very creative and has a good imagination. I think part *& why* the Indian killed the Hank brothers was because Hannie covered him back up with dirt, Hannie never told anybody and she moved her garden somewhere else. At first I didn't get it but *I'm very happy that you read it again!* then I read the story again and then I found out what was happening. I know somebody that lives on Galaxy Drive and Rock Road is just down the block. I wonder if *You could share the story with your friend.* they know the story. I wonder if that house in the story really is there or maybe it never ixzisted. Maybe that story is an old folk tale that has been past on for a long time between the families. I liked the story. ☺

4.3 *A fourth grader's journal entry and his teacher's questions and comments in the margin.*

they have read and to make connections with their own lives. Rebecca, a sixth grade teacher, had her students read folktales from around the world as part of a unit called "The Human Experience." She asked her students to share insights and personal reflections in their journals. Missy's entry in Figure 4.2 shows the connections she made between the motivating forces that shape the lives of all people, past and present. Rebecca's one word comment, "Powerful. . ." reinforces Missy's thoughtful observation.

These journals also allow students to voice their thoughts about authors' styles and to wonder about things that they might not normally share in class discussions. The entry in Figure 4.3 was written by a fourth grade student who was studying local his-tory in social studies. He had just read a story written by a local author and set in his community. The student recognizes the author's creativity, gives his own interpreta-tion to the story and wonders about the exact house in which the story took place. He notes also that he had to reread the story in order to understand it. His teacher, Julie, reinforces this as an effective comprehen-sion tool and poses questions to him in the margin of his journal.

Content of Responses

The content of students' literature response journals can help you assess and develop their reading abilities and behaviors. Pat-terns of similar responses in journals can alert you to students who need to broaden and extend the way they are looking at and experiencing literature.

For example, entries like the one in Figure 4.4 can alert you to comprehension problems. This seventh grade student would benefit from a small group discussion or a conference with his teacher, Barbara, to talk about Nigeria—the setting for the story, *The Joys of Motherhood* by Buchi Emecheta (George Braziller, 1988). By better understanding Nnu Ego, the main character, her struggle with an overbearing husband, and the value system of her tribe where failure in marriage could bring shame to her family and the village, the student can begin to reflect on how she feels about Nnu Ego's experience and can make connections to similar issues in her own culture.

4.4 A seventh grader's journal entry and his teacher's written response.

The kinds of responses your students write about the stories and books they read will vary. The following list of potential elements in student responses, not in a hierarchical order, gives you an idea of this range. Julie, the teacher who responded in the margins of the journal entry in Figure 4.3, could use the following criteria for identifying elements of this student's response. Check marks indicate which elements were included in the student's entry.

Elements of Written Response to Literature

☑ Identifies feelings story elicits.

☑ Identifies important information in story.

☐ Retells or summarizes story.

☑ Connects own experiences to story.

☑ Connects other books/authors to story/author.

☑ States opinion or preference and provides support.

☑ Interprets author's meaning.

☑ Analyzes aspects of setting, plot, characters or theme.

☐ Analyzes literary style.

☐ Identifies theme or generalizes to the larger world.

☐ Makes predictions or hypotheses.

☑ Asks questions.

When using a checklist such as this, look for elements that are not checked and frame your written responses to students in ways that will help them think about the story differently and might elicit these types of responses in future entries.

Integrating Response Journals With Language Learning and Literature

Journals are often part of reading-writing classrooms. They can also provide a framework for classroom instruction that integrates language learning and language use around literature. Reading-writing workshops have several components that do not always occur in the same day; independent reading and writing, literature discussion lessons, and skills lessons. Literature response journals can help make connections among these components—as independent writing to accompany reading, as sources of material to share in discussions, and as indicators of student strengths and needs in reading and writing to direct skills lessons. Students can write in their journals daily, on days when discussion groups meet, or in some combination to vary the procedure.

To get response journals off to a successful start in your classroom, begin by reading literature to your students that has potential for powerful responses. Tips for choosing literature include:

1. Choose books you know and like. Your enthusiasm for a favorite book will show and is contagious. Your students may catch your enthusiasm and make the transfer when writing in their journals.

2. Choose books that reinforce and add depth to a current content area unit or area of study. You can make connections for your students as they listen and invite them to make their own in their journals.

3. Ask students for suggestions. When you use their favorite authors and ideas, you invest your students in the stories you read and the journal entries they write, as well.

4. Choose books in which main characters are approximately the same age as your students. Younger students understand and appreciate more difficult chapter books that they can not read themselves, as long as the characters are about their age or they can relate to the setting and situation.

5. Share picture books with students of all ages. Read-alouds are worthwhile and satisfying experiences at all grade levels. Today's picture books deal with sophisticated themes and topics that are appreciated by older as well as younger students. In fact, many picture books contain difficult vocabulary and concepts that are best shared with both younger and older audiences through oral reading.

The following list includes selected read-alouds that can be used to launch writing in response journals:

For Young Readers

Wagon Wheels by Barbara Brenner (HarperCollins, 1984). Three young black brothers follow a map to their father's homestead on the Western Plains and endure storms, fire, and starvation to achieve their dream.

Trumpet of the Swan by E.B. White (HarperCollins, 1970). Louis, a voiceless trumpeter swan, learns to read, write, and play the trumpet which bring him fame, fortune, and fatherhood.

The Christmas Cup by Nancy Patterson (Orchard, 1988). Eight year-old Megan and her grandmother secretly collect coins in a cup and decide who will receive their anonymous gift.

And the Green Grass Grew All Around: Folk Poetry From Everyone by Alvin Schwartz (HarperCollins, 1992). An entertaining collection of folk poetry to be read out loud and enjoyed.

The Moonbow of Mr. B. Jones by Patrick Lewis (Knopf, 1992). A young boy learns to believe in magic when a peddler visits a small montain town to sell his wares and brings with him wonder and miracles.

Amazing Grace by Mary Hoffman (Dial, 1991). Grace, a young black girl, triumphs over racial and gender stereotyping.

For Middle Readers

In the Year of the Boar and Jackie Robinson by Betty Bao Lord (Trumpet, 1987). A young Chinese girl emigrates to New York in 1947 and assimilates into a strange new culture prompting discussion of culture, discrimination, and stereotyping.

The Apple and the Arrow: The Legend of William Tell by Mary and Conrad Buff (Scholastic, 1993). The famous Swiss legend told from the point of view of Tell's 12 year-old son, Walter, as the concept of freedom is explored.

Weasel by Cynthia DeFelice (Macmillan, 1990). Young Nathan and his sister, Molly, search for their father in the 1839 Ohio wilderness and meet a man the Shawnee

Indians call Weasel in this spellbinding story that spurs thinking about treatement of Native Americans.

Missing May by Cynthia Rylant (Orchard, 1992). This book is about twelve year-old Summer's grief, loss, learning, and love as a result of her Aunt May's death.

The Dark-Thirty: Southern Tales of the Supernatural by Patricia McKissack (Knopf, 1992). These tales of the supernatural, based on African American history and culture are riveting read-alouds.

For Older Readers

My Brother Sam Is Dead by James L. Collier (Scholastic, 1993). During the Revolutionary War, a family struggles with the country's and their own conflict between Loyalists and Patriots, and an adolescent boy acquires wisdom as a result.

A Stranger At Greene Knowe by Lucy Boston (Harcourt, 1989). Set in Africa and England with two main characters, a boy and a gorilla, this exciting story stimulates thinking about refugees, friendship, and humanity.

The Adventures of Ulysses by Bernard Evslyn (Scholastic, 1992). The Greek leader encounters Cyclops, the beautiful sorceress Circe and other trials as he avoids the anger of the gods.

When the Road Ends by Jean Thesman (Houghton Mifflin, 1992). Endurance, respect, and caring are themes in this story of a childlike adult and three misfit children who manage to survive and grow one summmer when they find themselves on their own.

This Same Sky: A Collection of Poems From Around the World Ed. Naomi Nye. (Four Winds, 1992). Beautiful poems by 129 contemporary poets from 68 countries are arranged according to themes like "Families," "Losses" and "Human Mysteries."

Dancing Carl by Gray Paulson (Scholastic, 1993). This is a moving remembrance of a real man who has a real impact on the lives of two 12 year-olds.

Books About Read-Alouds

Hey! Listen To This: Stories To Read Aloud Ed. Jim Trelease. (Penguin, 1992). A collection of mostly self-contained stories and some excerpted chapters with background information about each story and author.

The New Read Aloud Handbook by Jim Trelease. (Penguin, 1993). A book about how reading aloud stimulates language and learning with annotations of books for sharing orally with all ages.

Books Kids Will Sit Still For by Judy Freeman. (Bowker, 1990) An annotated bibliography of more than 2,000 titles including picture books, fiction, non-fiction, poetry, and folklore. Includes how-tos for storytelling, extension activites, and suggestions for creative drama.

Tips For Success

1. Some students seem to need the stimulus of a question to answer in order to get started with response journals. Occasionally, asking a question related to something specific that students have just read makes sense. For example, ask:

- How did the story make you feel?
- What did it remind you of?
- What was your favorite (least favorite) part? Why?
- What might happen next?
- Was your prediction accurate? Why or why not?
- Do you like the story? Why or why not?
- What lesson does the story hold?
- What insights into your own life does the story suggest?
- How is the main character similar to you?
- Do you agree or disagree with what the main character did?
- What have you learned about yourself as a reader?
- What would you like to do to become a better reader?

Remember, though, that if you always ask questions you may lead your students and in so doing they lose the opportunity to freely respond to what touches them about what they are reading.

2. Modelling is one of the most important aspects of successful literature response journal use. When you read, write entries in your journal, and share them with your students, you provide a model of literature response. In fact, when journals aren't going well and students are not interested in writing or are not interacting personally with their reading, sharing your responses with students can have an impact. Some teachers read their entries and some use overhead projec-

tors to show students what they have written and how it looks. Teachers who use this strategy report that students imitate both the substance and form of their modelled entries.

3. Another way to encourage thoughtful entries is for you to respond in writing to what your students write. The way you reply to your students is important in determining what and how they write in their journals in the future. Your responses must not criticize, but rather must establish that you appreciate your students' opinions, regardless of whether or not you agree with them. Supportive, nonevaluative comments and questions have the best results. You should be aware that your replies can help students develop their reading abilities as well as deepen their understanding of literature. Following are suggestions to guide your responses (Wolman-Bonilla, 1991), with possible teacher-replies to the student response in Figure 4.3 written about *The Joys of Motherhood* in italics:

- Share your own ideas and responses. (*As a wife and mother, my heart ached for Nnu Ego and the hurt and embarrassment she must have felt at the hands of her husband.*)

- Provide information. (*In Nnu Ego's tribe, if your marriage fails you bring shame to your family.*)

- Develop students' awareness of reading strategies. (*Now that you know a little more about the chapter, read it again to see if it makes more sense to you and let me know if you're still*

confused. *What did you learn by re-reading?*)

- Develop students' awareness of literary techniques. (*What's your guess as to why the author made the comparison she did in this chapter?*)

- Model the way you want students to elaborate their responses. (*I agree with you, it was a confusing chapter. I remember having feelings that were in conflict, as Nnu Ego did. But, I would have reacted very differently to being hit over the head with a guitar! Would you? Of course, the culture of that Nigerian tribe dictated her response.*)

- Challenge students to think in new ways. (*I wonder if she will change and her behavior will be more "liberated" by the end of the story?! Do you think our unit's organizing idea, "Conflict requires resolution," is true for Nnu Ego?*)

4. Some teachers write a letter a week to each student, writing in a few journals each day so that the job is not overwhelming. Other teachers occasionally write brief comments in journal margins, like Julie did in Figure 4.2, finding that a few phrases or a question here and there are enough to keep students on target. Others, write longer responses, as Barbara did in Figure 4.3.

5. Occasionally ask students to share entries with each other. Sharing responses allows students to see how their peers feel about stories they are reading and hear how their peers respond in their journals. Allowing students to share responses:

- encourages discussion;
- confirms and validates opinions and feelings;
- exposes a range of ideas;
- extends understanding and appreciation;
- reinforces learning;
- builds a community of readers who have shared knowledge and experiences.

6. To encourage individual accountability, you can ask your students to keep track of what they read and evaluate the books and their entries. Some teachers ask students to record daily the number of pages they read. Often, students keep a monthly list in the back of their journals of the books they have read. You might also have students record, for each book, the author and genre or type of book it is and their rating of it, using for example, a 5-point scale from 5—"Awesome!" to 1—"Awful." Have students write a sentence or two to support their ratings.

Students can also evaluate the quantity, quality, and regularity of their entries using, for example, a 3-point scale 3—"Excellent," 2—"Average" or 1—"Weak."

References

Flitterman-King, S. (1988). The role of the response journal in active reading. *The Quarterly of the National Writing Project and the Center for the Study of Writing*, 10, 4–11.

Hancock, M.R. (1992). Literature response journals: Insights beyond the printed page. *Language Arts*, 69 (1), 36–42.

Rosenblatt, L.M. (1985). The transactional theory of the literary work: Implications for research. In C.R. Cooper (Ed.) *Researching Response to Literature and the Teaching of Literature: Points of Departure*. (pp. 33–53). Norwood, NJ: Ablex.

Wolman-Bonilla, J. (1991). *Response Journals: Inviting Students to Think and Write About Literature*. New York: Scholastic.

CHAPTER 5

Learning Log

Learning logs are a type of journal in which students write informally about what they have learned.

When you introduce learning logs to students at any grade level, tell them they can use these logs to record newly acquired knowledge in a content area such as science or social studies, or as a place to respond in a more general way to anything they have learned. Tompkins (1990) and Romano (1987) identify several purposes for this type of informal writing, including to:

- prepare to learn;
- record observations and experiences;
- explore thinking;
- personalize learning;
- struggle with difficult ideas; think independently;
- wonder and engage the imagination;
- share experiences with a trusted reader.

Learning logs allow students to summarize lessons, react to class activities, keep observational records of class experiments, ask questions, link present knowledge with new knowledge, reflect on what they have learned, identify problems with their own learning, and dialogue with a teacher or other students about interesting or confusing subject matter.

Like literature response journals, learning logs offer opportunities to personally process information. When students write about something in their own words, they make ideas their own. Learning logs provide records that can be revisited and reread, or studied for tests. They can be springboards for further learning.

5.1 *This first grader spells "milk" and "ice cream" correctly in her learning log.*

5.2 *The teacher wrote what the child dictated under his picture and also wrote a note about the picture.*

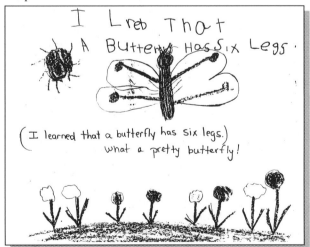

Finally, learning logs offer access to your students' learning processes. Used as diagnostic tools, they can help you establish the focus of future lessons and also help you know what needs to be retaught to which students.

Implementing Learning Logs

In Primary Grade Classes

Young children can use learning logs to draw as well as write about what they learn. Sue, a first grade teacher, encouraged her students to draw first and then write about daily lessons in a science unit on change. She discovered the benefit of leaving science vocabulary on the blackboard after she finished teaching—children's learning logs often contained vocabulary from the lesson that was spelled correctly (Figures 5.1–5.2). Sue read children's entries and dialogued with them in their journal. Sue provided a model for future entries by having children read what they wrote and then transcribing what they said using standard spelling. Her children enjoyed occasionally sharing their entries with buddies, with the group at their table, or with the entire class.

Sue felt the learning logs helped her key in to children's various stages of literacy development. For example, one child composed a string of letters "A i Y N W A H" to represent what she had learned, showing very early invented spelling. The child did not appear to be able to match the letters she had written with the words she dictated, "The caterpillar, he climbed into his chrysalis. And then he got wrecked. And he was a butterfly." Sue concluded that this child was beginning to make a match between spoken and written language, but that the match was not yet developed to the point where the child could represent individual sounds with letters.

Jane found learning logs to have a double advantage in her second grade. Her students' entries told her what they were learning throughout their science unit on the weather and also what they wanted to learn. In Figure 5.3 a child tells Jane that he has learned the water cycle and where rain goes. He also lets Jane know that he still wonders about thunder and lightening. This learning log gave Jane a possible direction for planning for future instruction.

In Middle Grade Classes

In third grade, Pat's students used learning logs to document what they were learning during a unit of study that had an organizing idea and title of "It's All Around Us All the Time: Weather." The children called the journals their "Lab Books" and Pat used them as a way to stretch her students' thinking (Figure 5.4).

Diane and Sandy, team-teaching a unit on food chains to fourth graders, made a learning log for each student in their class. On the cover of each journal, a yellow sun represented the unit's organizing idea, "Let's Eat A Sunbeam!" (Figure 5.5). These teachers intentionally did not tell children what it meant, challenging them to figure out the meaning as they learned about food chains.

5.3 A second grader writes about what she has learned and identifies what she still wants to learn.

5.4 Pat asks one of her second graders a question in the learning log.

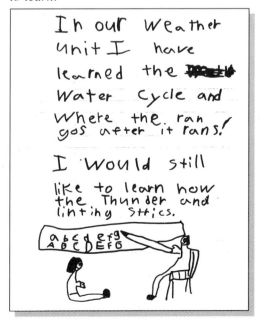

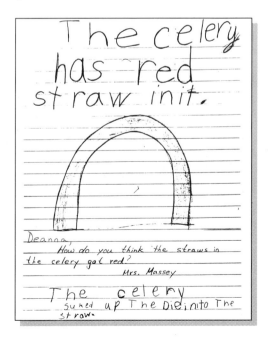

5.5 The cover of Michael's learning log.

Michael's and Erin's entries (Figure 5.6–5.8) show how they dialogued back and forth with their teachers about the content of lessons. Michael's question in Figure 5.7 seems more for the purpose of demonstrating his own knowledge than to gain new knowledge. Or, it may show that he was grappling with confusing material. Erin answered Mrs. Mannix's question and asked a question in Figure 5.8 to get to know her teacher better.

Most students figured out what the title of the log meant by the end of the unit. In one

---

11/8

Today I learned about different Kinds of chains. I also did food Chains. Timber Rattlesnake (crotalus horridus) eats mice/frogs, which eat flies, which eat small organisms.

Michael,
You seem to know a lot about snakes. Do you like to learn about them? yes
— Mrs. Mannix

11/14/89

Today I learned about Chlorophyl and Photosynthesis. We are also doing an experiment.

Shark → Mackerel → Prawn → Phyroplankton

It will be interesting to see what happens to each of the plants. Thanks for the food chain. In a few weeks we will be studying about ocean food chains. You can share this one then. What is a prawn? A prawn is a mrs. Whitehouse shrimp- like crustacean, but is larger.

5.6 Michael and his teachers write in his learning log.

12/8
Today we wrote letters + did stuff about Borneo. I have a question for you to answer.

Do sharks live in fresh water?
A. yes
B. no
C. sometimes

Answer— my answer is sometimes.
I Know there are sharks who live in the sea (saltwater), & I think there are freshwater sharks, too.
Have you ever seen a shark? I saw some at the aquarium at Baltimore and they were very large.
When I was in Charleston a few years ago I saw two dolphins swimming while I was out for a boat ride. I think I'd like to see a whale someday, but I don't know if I'd like to see a shark outside of in aquarium!
Mrs. Mannix

5.7 In his learning log, Michael asks the teacher a question related to the science unit and she answers.

40

> Erin,
> I like strawberries, too — especially right after they've been picked — yum!
> Can you think of an example of more than one animal eating the same food? For example, can you think of another animal besides a human that would eat an apple?
> Have a nice day! Don't forget your food list!
> Mrs. Manny
>
> Humans eat apples and food deers eat them. Today we learned that if one part of the food chain dies the whole food chain changes. Also humans can affect the food chains. Lots of food chains put together = a food web. That's neat. Have a great day. What is your favorite animal?
>
> I like dogs and owls. Your plant seems to be doing better, don't you think? Your log entries are very good. Have you thought about what "Let's Eat a Sunbeam" means? What is your favorite animal?
> Mrs. Whitehouse

5.8 Erin summarizes what she has learned in her log and asks the teacher a personal question.

> 3/3 I learned my brain would work but I didn't lett it took.
> Jolene — I'm sorry you were having a tough time. Let's work together to get "your brain working" again!
> Your first revision is correct. I think you are on the right track now.
> Ms. Bailey
>
> 3/6 Today I learned how it would be user to use a check list so you can pass a test on the computed test it would be a lot easlry to read or so you pass. I think it will be easier.
> Jolene — you did a great job working as a group member and with coming up with ideas. I'm glad you brought up spelling and word spacing especially. I'm glad you think they will help. We'll try it on the next essay.
>
> 3/6 To conontrate harder on the asseys and I will do better.
> Jolene — what is it we discussed that you could concentrate on or think about that would help get your essay organized in your head? Ms. Bailey
>
> 3/15 I promble would pass the test on it know I now the steps to it.
> Jolene — you do seem to have the steps down pat for using the outline to write. Now I want you to tell me what you can do before you start to write that can help you organize some ideas.
> Ms. Bailey

5.9 Jolene, a ninth grader, discusses her own learning with her teacher.

of his last entries, Shawn wrote "Let's eat a sunbeam means. A producer gets eaten by a herbivore and the h. gets eaten by an cornivor or a omnivore. And this means it's a food chain. I learned about rats that parachuted into Borneo, And DDT. I like this class a lot. I sure had a lot of fun."

With Special Needs Students

Joylyn, a junior high school resource room teacher, used a learning log to encourage self-reflection and to make learning personal for her students. She was working with several students to help them monitor and edit their own writing in preparation for a writing competency test. Jolene was beginning to make a conscious effort to help herself by using an editing check list to revise her writing (Figure 5.9). Joylyn's comments acknowledge Jolene's frustrations and support her in her attempts to focus and concentrate. In their dialogue, Joylyn tries to help Jolene think for herself and apply what she knows when she is writing an essay.

Tips For Success

After using learning logs for a few weeks, teachers often report that the logs get stale and students lose interest in them. How do you sustain motivation for learning logs? Brewster (1988) suggests creativity and variety, for example:

1. Have students alternate a week of knowledge entries and a week of opinion entries.

2. Allow older students to use drawings instead of words occasionally.

3. Keep a class log on a bulletin board having a different student responsible for each day's entry.

4. Have students keep a double entry journal with one side of the page for recording new knowledge and the other for reacting personally to it.

5. Take a week or two off.

6. Use dittoed log sheets illustrated by a students.

7. Allow use of pens with scented ink or colored felt-tip markers.

References

Brewster, M. (1988). Ten ways to revive tired learning logs. *English Journal,* 77 (2), p. 57.

Romano, T. (1987). *Clearing the Way: Working With Teenage Writers.* Portsmouth, NH: Heinemann.

Tompkins, G. (1990). *Teaching Writing: Balancing Process and Product.* Columbus, OH: Merrill.

CHAPTER 6

Dialogue Journal

The dialogue journal is designed to create interactions in which two minds can unite to bring about new understanding, new ideas, new possibilities. A dialogue means continuity of discussion, until the meaning of a topic has been worked out; dialogue means unpredictability and novelty. . . (p. 54, Staton, 1984).

The dialogue journal is a written conversation between teacher and student that occurs regularly, sometimes daily but usually two or three times a week. Students write about topics of their own choice and teachers write back, responding to what students have written, often introducing new topics. Teachers share observations and opinions, extend or elaborate on student entries, seek and provide clarification when they are unsure of what a student means, answer student questions, and ask questions of their own.

Characteristics and Benefits

You may find it helpful to be aware of the dialogue journal's distinctive characteristics before implementing the activity in your classroom. These journals can be time consuming when used with all students at once but as you'll see, the benefits are a big plus. Dialogue journals are:

Interactive: Dialogue journals allow you and your students to socialize together and learn about each other's personal thoughts, tastes, and opinions. You are equal partners in this reading-writing exchange.

Cumulative: This on-going collection of entries is like an extended conversation that isn't always possible in the typical classroom. You and a student can converse about a single topic for an extended time or cover a number of different topics.

Self-initiated: Both you and your students are free to choose what you write about. Either of you can respond to an entry in depth or ignore it and move on to another topic, just as you might in a spoken conversation.

Functional: You and your students use language for real purposes. You communicate with each other as you share and learn.

Why use dialogue journals with your students? Dialogue journals have many benefits which you'll want to be aware of as you think about exploring this type of journal further. You can use dialogue journals to:

• individualize learning;

• personalize writing instruction;

• provide accurate models for students to imitate;

• develop writing fluency through practice;

• provide a nonthreatening and free context for writing;

• build motivation and confidence for writing;

• provide an authentic audience;

• validate self-expression;

• build strong interpersonal bonds;

• connect reading, writing, and thinking naturally.

Getting Started

Some teachers begin the school year by having their students keep personal journals in which students write about topics they choose. Once students have kept this type of journal for a time, you can introduce them to the dialogue journal. Either ask for volunteers or tell your students that you would like to begin having a written conversation with each of them in their journal.

Here are a few specific ideas to help you get started:

1. Give each student a journal with lined paper, ask that they each purchase one and bring one to school, or make your own journals. Lined paper makes writing neater and easier to read. Be sure to give them a chance to decorate and personalize their covers.

2. Set aside a certain time to write and establish how long your students will write. A regular time and day builds consistency. Usually 10 minutes is a good amount of time to start with. As students become more proficient at writing, you can extend the amount of time.

3. Establish a minimum number of sentences or words so that students get into the habit of writing entries of enough length that they can develop their thoughts. This is less important as your students get into dialogue journals. Of course, with beginning writers or students who are just learning English, you need to be sensitive to their abilities.

4. Identify a place in your room where students should put their journals when they have finished writing, for example, on a shelf or in a bag that you normally take home with you. You may also want students to mark their last entry with a book mark to save you time when you want to read and reply to their entries.

5. Reply to students as you would if you were having a social conversation. Get

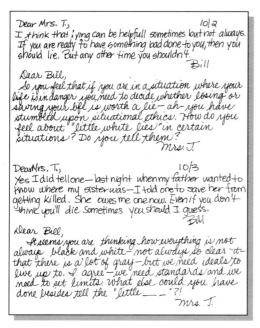

Dear Mrs. T.,   10/2
I think that lying can be helpfull sometimes but not always. If you are ready to have something bad done to you, then you should lie. But any other time you shouldn't.
Bill

Dear Bill,
So you feel that if you are in a situation where your life is in danger you need to decide whether losing or saving your life is worth a lie — ah — you have stumbled upon situational ethics. How do you feel about "little white lies" in certain situations? Do you tell them?
Mrs. J.

Dear Mrs. T.,   10/3
Yes I did tell one — last night when my father wanted to know where my sister was — I told one to save her from getting killed. She owes me one now. Even if you don't think you'll die sometimes you should I guess.
Bill

Dear Bill,
It seems you are thinking how everything is not always black and white, not always so clear "it — that there is a lot of gray — but we need ideals to live up to. I agree — we need standards and we need to set limits. What else could you have done besides tell the "little ___ "?!
Mrs. J.

6.1 Mrs. T. dialogues with Bill about ethics and helps him reexamine his beliefs.

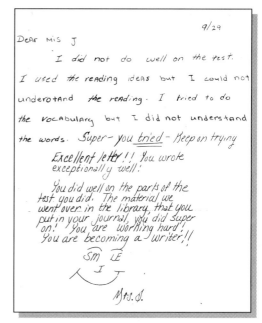

9/29
Dear Mis J.
I did not do well on the test. I used the reading ideas but I could not understand the reading. I tried to do the vocabulary but I did not understand the words. Super - you tried - Keep on trying
Excellent letter!! You wrote exceptionally well.
You did well on the parts of the test you did. The material we went over in the library, that you put in your journal, you did super on! You are working hard! You are becoming a writer!!
SMILE
Mrs. J.

6.2 Mrs. J. reinforces the student for trying and for her good work, at the same time reminding her of how the journal helped her.

out of your teacher role for awhile, be yourself, and enjoy the person-to-person dialogue. For example, don't just ask questions or give lots of information, as this will stifle conversations you have with your students.

At first, your dialogue journals can be personal and unrelated to school, if this is what you and your students prefer. Writing about family, friends, and life issues is an excellent way to get to know your students. Bill, a ninth grade student, dialogued with his teacher, Mrs. T., about the ethics of lying (Figure 6.1). Through their journal conversations, Bill's teacher helped him extend his thinking. He realized that he really didn't live by his first statement about lies. In another student's journal (Figure 6.2), Jan, a high school resource room teacher, praised a student for trying on a test and for a well written letter. Jan also directed the student's attention to the role her journal played in her learning.

Once students are comfortable with journal writing you can give them opportunities to reflect on what they are reading by combining the dialogue journal with the literature response journal. In this combined journal, you and your students can converse together about books they are reading. Some teachers ask their students to write to them once a week about the books they are reading (Atwell, 1987). In this way, you learn much about how each student is interacting with the story and author, and you have an opportunity to nudge students along to make interpretations and insights that might not be possible without your input.

Dialogue Journals for Special Students

As well as being a satisfying and effective form of writing that is helpful for students who seem to have no obvious special needs, dialogue journal writing is useful for teachers of students with special needs. You can use dialogue journals to individualize writing instruction by providing a model of standard spelling and vocabulary that fits the strengths, needs, and interests of each student.

Research supports using dialogue journals with students who have special needs. Dialogue journals used with students who have limited English proficiency (LEP) can enhance their oral and written language acquisition (Peyton & Reed, 1990). Other studies show that dialogue journals motivate students who have learning disabilities to write and provide them with practice in writing (Gaustad & Messenheimer-Young, 1991; Staton & Tyler, 1987). They are also effective in developing the thinking, reading, and writing of students with hearing impairments (Staton, 1985).

Responding to Student Entries

What and how much do you need to write to students in dialogue journals? If you think of this type of journal as a written conversation, your question is easily answered. When you talk to a friend or an acquaintance, you usually pursue whatever topic they introduce. As you talk, you also initiate new topics or interject them when it is appropriate.

Written conversations follow the same guidelines. When you write, you respond to the topic that has been introduced and you initiate or interject new topics when it seems natural. And just as when you talk, the amount you have to say varies, depending on how much time you have and on how fluent you are.

Remember to write in complete sentences because this will force you to avoid "quickie" comments that curb a conversation and don't really extend dialogue. A good rule of thumb about entry length is: The entries you write, in most cases, should match students' literacy levels and usually do not need to be longer than students' entries. At the same time, try to extend your language just far enough beyond students' that they are challenged. If you write too much, a student who is not a fluent writer may be overwhelmed and have trouble responding. If you write too little, your remarks may be superficial. So, you need to match what you say and how much you write to each student and the topic or message.

Tips For Success

The biggest obstacle to the success of this type of journal writing is time. Dialogue journals require a considerable time commitment on your part. Are the paybacks worth the large blocks of time they obviously require? Many teachers feel they are well worth the time and effort they invest. There are several things you can do to manage:

1. Begin dialogue journals with only a few students at first, perhaps one small group, so you feel good about writing entries before you begin to write to the whole class.

2. Look at only a few journals a day, instead of reading and replying to each journal every day. Do this by giving each of your student journals a number, 1–25 for example, and then assign 1–5 to Monday, 6–10 to Tuesday, and so on. With this system you can read and reply to just 5 journals a day.

3. Dialogue with half your class at a time. For example, you can write to half your class for one month and the other half for the next month, and so on, or for shorter or longer time periods, as makes sense for you and your students. For young children, two weeks may be long enough. During the month that half the class is not writing to you in dialogue journals, they may opt to keep another kind of journal described in this book, for example, a personal journal, a writer's journal, a go-home journal, or a buddy journal.

4. Dialogue with all the students in your class, but only write back and forth two or three times a week. Once you have dialogue journals going and students are writing in them regularly, you may want to write only once a week.

5. Combine or creatively blend any of these suggestions to best fit your situation and your students' needs.

6. Keep a class record sheet, perhaps by month, of who is doing what and for how long, so that you have a plan and things don't get out of hand. Post this record or plan and involve students in keeping it to give them an active role in journaling and to allow them to see the big picture for the class as a whole.

References

Atwell, N. (1987). *In the Middle: Writing, Reading and Learning With Adolescents.* Portsmouth, NH: Heinemann.

Gaustad, M. G., & Messenheimer-Young, T. (1991). Dialogue journals for students with learning disabilities. *Teaching Exceptional Children*, 23, 2, 28–32.

Peyton, J.K., & Reed, L. (1990). *Dialogue Journal Writing With Non-Native English Speakers: A Handbook for Teachers.* Alexandria, VA: TESOL.

Staton, J. (1985). Using dialogue journals for developing thinking, reading, and writing with hearing-impaired students. *Volta Review*, 87, 5, 127–153.

Staton, J. (1984). The power of responding in dialogue journals. In *The Journal Book*, Ed. T. Fulwiler (pp. 47–63). Portsmouth, NH: Heinemann.

Staton, J., & Tyler, D. (1987). Dialogue journal use with learning-disabled students. *The Pointer*, 32, 1, 4–8.

Buddy Journal

What's the best thing about buddy journals? After writing in them for four weeks, this is how a group of third graders responded to that question: (see also Fig. 7.1)

We got to share our thoughts.

We got a chance to meet people.

Reading what my buddy wrote.

Questions you could ask.

Sharing secrets.

Making new friends.

We could pick a name out of a hat.

The mystery of not knowing what your buddy wrote.

Finding out stuff about other people.

Writing to someone you really don't know.

Understanding their problems.

We got to write about what we want.

Talking to people by writing not by mouth.

A new way in communicating.

A buddy journal is a diary that a pair of students keeps together (Bromley, 1989). In this variation of the dialogue journal, students write back and forth to each other. The buddy journal is similar to an oral conversation two children might have with one another. It is a natural way to read and write in a purposeful and personally meaningful context as students interact socially.

Buddy journals require students to read their partners' entries in order to write responses or give feedback (Figure 7.2). Students usually generate their own topics and entries are not evaluated or graded by the teacher. Writing in buddy journals serves students' own purposes rather than those of the teacher, since students ask and answer their own questions, describe feelings, share interests and activities, make requests, dis-

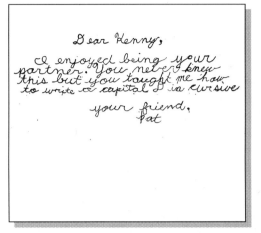

Dear Kenny,

I enjoyed being your partner. You never knew this but you taught me how to write a capital D in cursive

your friend,
Pat

7.1 *Pat tells Kenny how he felt about buddy journals and thanks him for the good handwriting model he provided.*

12-2
My new sister is a pain she wakes me up at night all the time. motly at 3:30 in the morning Then she gas back to sleep and wakes me up at 7:00.

She shire is a pane. you stile love her dont you? do you have eney older sisters or brothers?

12-6
my mom dos't pay any atenchen to me she pay most atenchen to Jennifer.

thats not far is it? if she pase more ateng to deannifer.

7.2 *Michele gives Krista support and sympathy in her buddy journal entries.*

cuss ideas, and develop relationships with each other.

Buddy journals are useful at all grade levels and for a variety of purposes, including with young children who enjoy drawing, scribbling, and sharing the beginnings of writing with one another. You can use buddy journals within individual classrooms, between classrooms of students at the same grade level, or among different grade levels to establish friendships and build a sense of community in a school. If you teach second-language learners, you can link these students in buddy journals with students whose first language is English and who serve as models and mentors. As students interact together in buddy journals, literacy grows, relationships develop, and students learn about each other as cultural, ethnic, and racial barriers disappear.

More detailed descriptions of buddy journals in a variety of classroom settings follow, including at different grade levels, with special needs students, and with ESL students.

Kindergarten Buddies

Betsy introduced buddy journals to her kindergarten students telling them they would each make a new friend in the kindergarten class across the hall through their journals. She and her colleague matched children according to who they believed would work well together, for example, children who were beginning writers and those with similar interests. They agreed to exchange journals twice a week.

Betsy helped her children make journals by stapling wallpaper covers to several sheets of wide-lined paper, with space at the top for picture-drawing. She printed both students' names on each journal cover and let children decorate the covers. Betsy's students drew and wrote in their journals just before lunch

My name is StACI.
I like the computer.

7.3 Staci's teacher writes Staci's words in her buddy journal.

My name is Jenna

I like to Play Computer
Wontto getto ge

Jenna

7.4 Jenna writes her own buddy journal entry to Staci.

and shared their entries with each other after lunch twice a week. After each sharing session, they sent the journals across the hall so their buddies could read, draw, and write in them.

The range of writing ability in the two classrooms was wide, with only a few emergent writers and most children unable to write, but almost all eager to draw and scribble. Betsy usually directed the journal activities. At first she had children draw pictures of themselves and what they liked to do. For several children who were not ready to write, like Staci, Betsy transcribed their words for them (Figures 7.3 and 7.5). Some children, like Jenna, wrote their own entries (Figures 7.4 and 7.6) or wrote letters or scribbles to stand for words that Betsy also transcribed.

Jenna,
Come play
dress up.
Staci

7.5 Staci responds to Jenna with a request.

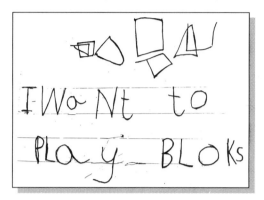

7.6 *Jenna tells Staci what she wants to do when they get together.*

Through trial and error, Betsy found that several things helped make buddy journals a success. She discovered that when the two classes shared an activity together, it gave impetus to the drawing and writing. So, once a week, half Betsy's class went to the other kindergarten, and vice versa, where buddies participated together in an activity in one of the class center areas.

Betsy found many opportunities to reinforce literacy learning and knowledge as children proudly shared their journal pages. She publicly noted words that children tried to spell themselves, realistic pictures that some children drew, and children's abilities to "read" dictated words on the pages of their journals. Betsy and her colleague found journal writing to be an activity that worked best for short periods of time. They used it on and off during the year, matching different students each time.

To vary the activity, Betsy teamed up with a fourth grade teacher to pair their students in buddy journal writing. Together, older and younger buddies drew and wrote in their journals. Older students also read books to their kindergarten buddies. Both

7.7 *Addie draws a picture for Jessica in their journal.*

groups used literacy in meaningful ways and built friendships. Older students became responsible mentors, as well.

Second Grade Buddies

Kim used dialogue journal writing in September and October for about ten minutes three times a week as a way to get to know her students better and as a break in the morning between reading and math. She dialogued weekly with students in their journals and enjoyed the personal relationships the class established via the journals.

In November, she introduced buddy journals when her students were familiar with making entries and conversing with her in their dialogue journals. After describing the

7.8 Jessica writes a poem to Addie in their journal.

7.9 Addie meets a new word in the buddy journal and tells Jessica she will use the dictionary to find out its meaning.

procedure of swapping journals with a buddy, reading an entry, thinking about a response, and writing an entry in the buddy's journal, she asked for volunteers. Everyone volunteered and within a few minutes found a buddy. Two children did not at first have luck finding a partner, but Kim helped them find each other.

Children used the same journals in which they had been dialoguing with Kim. Most buddies eagerly wrote back and forth to each other for ten or fifteen minutes about three times a week.

Kim established a two-week time period for the first round of buddy journals. Since her students wrote in their journals three times a week, this allowed students to make entries in their journals one day, swap jour-

nals, and make entries in their buddies' journals the next day, and so on for for 6 days. So, each day at journal time, buddies swapped journals, read the last entry or entries, and added their own responses. After two weeks, buddies had the chance to change partners or return to a dialogue journal with Kim.

Third Grade Buddies

Some teachers match students for a specific purpose, as did Catherine and Sheila, two third-grade teachers who were both reading aloud the same book to their classes. One class heard a chapter from Elizabeth George Speare's book, *The Sign of the Beaver* (Houghton Mifflin, 1983) in the morning and the other heard the same chapter in the afternoon. The teachers paired children randomly for the most part, although some pairs were matched according to strengths and needs. Buddies made and illustrated their journals together.

Catherine and Sheila established rules for writing in buddy journals. They asked children to begin entries with "Dear_____," and end with "From" or "Your Buddy" or "Your Friend." They asked the children to write in cursive, to write about the story, and to use no "put-downs."

After reading a chapter, the morning class wrote reactions in their journals about what they had just heard. Catherine then sent the journals down the hall to Sheila's class. Shiela read the same chapter, then her

students responded to both the story and to their buddies' journal entries. Children could explore other topics as well, but were required to at least share and discuss their responses and interpretations of the oral reading. To give all students a chance to respond to their buddies' entries, the classes reversed the procedure after a period of time.

At first, things went well and even the most reluctant readers and writers were motivated by this project and wrote eagerly to their partners. Catherine and Sheila did encounter some problems, though. For example, some of the entries did not relate to the chapter or were very short. They began having children think of something specific that happened in the chapter, write about it, and then give a personal response, which

7.10 *Katie and Gada iron out details in* The Sign of the Beaver *and comment on each other's handwriting.*

7.11 *Katie and Gada share their opinions and questions about the chapter they heard and Katie reminds Gada to include a date on her entries.*

improved entries. Some buddies did not follow the "no put-down" rule. One, in particular, took offense when a name was misspelled and buddies began a verbal battle, insulting each other in their journal entries. When the teachers discovered this, they had the two buddies talk face-to-face to straighten out the misunderstanding. The teachers monitored journal entries more closely after that and the problem disappeared.

Buddy journals provided firsthand lessons about communication in Catherine's and Sheila's classes. When children's writing was sloppy, their buddies could not understand the messages. Since children were intent on being understood, they tried their hardest to write neatly and spell words correctly. At first some children had trouble

reading entries because of innacurate spelling, but when the teachers showed them how to sound out the invented spelling, they could usually understand what their buddies were trying to say. For children who requested a lot of help with spelling, Catherine and Sheila taight a mini-lesson on using existing environmental print, invented spelling, and the dictionary. Both teachers did help with confusing or messy entries.

Part way through the book, to vary the routine, Catherine and Sheila began assembling children on Friday afternoons to hear a chapter together and to encourage face-to-face interactions. To extend comprehension, one day buddies discussed the chapter and came up with five questions they had about the story, which they traded with

7.12 Katie refuses to answer Gada's questions until Gada responds to her previous question about liking fish.

7.13 The two girls make predictions about the story and Gada refuses to write longer paragraphs.

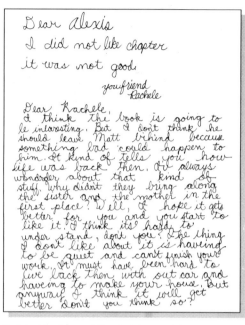

Dear Alexis
I did not like chapter
it was not good.
yourfriend
Rachele

Dear Rachele,
I think the book is going to
be interesting. But I don't think he
should leave Matt behind because
something bad could happen to
him. It kind of tells you how
life was back then. I always
wondered about that kind of
stuff. Why didn't they bring along
the sister and the mother in the
first place? Well, I hope it gets
better for you and you start to
like it. It's hard to
understand, don't you? The thing
I don't like about it is haveing
to be quiet and can't finish your
work. It must have been hard to
live back then with out car and
haveing to make your food. But
anyway I think it will get
better don't you think so?

7.14 *Alexis and Rachel have different opinions about the story.*

Dear alexis
I liked this chapter, if I
was matt I wood not
went to live alone. when
I oped are budd journal
and saw how much you
write I was shocked. I am
not telling you not to write so
much, you can write. how much
you went your friend Rachele

Dear Rachele,   Nov. 5
I liked that chapter too.
I think I know whats going to
happen next. how about you? I would
not like to be Matt either. I'm
really glad your starting to like
the book. I liked the other chapter
better. I wish we could right about
different things then the story, do you?
Your Friend,
Alexis

7.15 *Noting Alexis' long entry, Rachel writes more and Alex wishes she could write about other things, not just the story.*

another buddy pair and then tried to answer. As a large group, they shared and discussed answers to the difficult questions. On another Friday, buddies created character sketches together in the form of small books which they illustrated and put on a hall bulletin board. They did other activities together related to the story; they drew pictures, did creative role-playing, and wrote poetry as well.

Catherine and Sheila are enthusiastic about the learning that resulted from buddy journals. Their third graders had a richer experience with literature than they might have if they had only listened to the story with no peer interaction. As well, they learned to write clearly and legibly so that others could understand their thoughts and ideas. They also learned to share and to respect the opinions of others and work cooperatively.

Special Needs Buddies

Maryann's special class students avoided writing. Writing was difficult for them and they lacked motivation. She thought that buddy journals might furnish a way to make writing fun for them.

Maryann teaches a middle-school level, self-contained class of students who have learning disabilities and cognitive impairments. The IQ's of her 15 students ranged from the high 60's to mid 80's and their reading levels ranged from grades 1–4. Concern about her students' illegible handwriting and need to build fluency in their writing led Maryann to collaborate with a colleague who taught a similar but smaller and lower functioning group of students. These teachers decided to implement a buddy journal program to provide their students with a real purpose and peer audience for writing and to provide themselves with assessment data to guide future instruction. The specific objectives were for students to:

1. Practice literacy in a safe context.

2. Develop legibility in handwriting.

3. Build peer relationships.

Each teacher introduced buddy journals to her own group first. In introductory lessons, the buddy journal was compared to an oral conversation with a peer and a written letter to a faraway friend. Students brainstormed possible greetings, topics for messages, closings, and signatures. The teachers wrote illegible messages on the blackboard and led discussions of the importance of neatness. Each student in Maryann's class made a journal and listed topics on the inside back cover to use as a reference. Maryann also stapled a model handwriting guide to the back of each journal.

The teachers shared the objectives of the project with students and told them that entries would not be graded or corrected. They matched students who did not know each other and through discussion, established rules for journal writing:

1. Choose your own topics.

2. Write independently.

3. Spell words the best you can.

4. Do not write anything offensive.

5. No grades.

Each teacher modelled a journal entry. Then students began their correspondence. Students exchanged journals for 8 weeks, every other day or every third day, with 15–20 minutes a day spent reading and writing entries, which were only read by teachers at student request.

For the most part, students wrote about things that were important to them personally, such as hobbies and interests—collecting sports cards, hunting, fishing, personal grooming, attending dances, designing science projects, reading books, and playing video games. Several students used nicknames and drew pictures in their journals. Each day volunteers shared entries orally with the class. Motivation to read what their buddies wrote was high.

Legibility improved in most buddy journals, especially when one buddy drew attention to a problem:

I cannot read you wrighting. Could you right more clearly?

Improve on spelling please. I'll try harder on spelling to.

You have to start writing bigger because I can't really see your writing that good and I can't understand what you are saying.

When a buddy commented on handwriting, there was usually an attempt to write more neatly and a visible improvement in letter formation and spacing. Spelling remained inconsistent, with some students taking cues from their buddies' correct spellings and others ignoring it. Greetings and closings were also inconsistent. The teachers noted that in all journals, punctuation was omitted more often than it was appropriately used.

One friendship developed between a pair of girls who did not know each other initially. At first they did not seem to like each other, but within the pages of the journal discovered common interests. At first they shared factual information, but in later entries revealed personal things, explored their relationship, and even gave each other advice. A few weeks into the buddy journal project they began to sit together at lunch and the friendship began in earnest. A few selected parts of their later entries follow:

> . . .Why are you going out with duan he is a dunce he is going out with Sonia to. now that is grose. . .I thank you should brake up with duane. Why do you like duane?
> (Laurie)

Dear Laurie,
> Hi How are you Do you like me I like you a lot Your my best friend. . .
> (Tina)

Tina,
> I am sorry but I am not your best friend and you fare not mine. Tonya is my best friend. . .
> (Laurie)

> Hello, My best friend is Kristy she is like a sister to me of you do not like me that is find I dot rele cair You can be that way if you want to be
> (Tina)

> Way are you being mean to me? I did not do eny-thang fyou. I told you that I already had a best friend and it is the trooth. Me and Tonya are close and nothing is going to get in

oor way! way did you say I was you best friend if Kristy is? Dont be mean to me!
> (Laurie)

> Hi How are you i am not med at you no more I like you just for a friend that is if its ok with you. . .
> (Tina)

Maryann was pleased with the results of using buddy journals and felt her objectives were achieved. For teachers trying a similar approach to encouraging writing, she recommends:

- modelling appropriate entries to show students many examples of the form and content of good entries;
- monitoring content to keep it appropriate;
- providing instruction in spelling and punctuation to help students with learning disabilities acquire these skills. Using copies of actual journal entries without student names, or the overhead projector, to share, demonstrate, and discuss proper spelling and punctuation might be more relevant and interesting than skillsheets or workbook pages;
- allowing time for socializing together to help maintain enthusiasm. Time spent interacting together can enrich peer relationships and make topic choice in writing to each other easier;
- pairing special students with students in regular classrooms, too, to help special needs students make friends and become accepted by other peers as well.

4\6

Dear Diyar,
How is E.S.L.?
Do you like school?
Who is your faviort
t'eacher. See you
tomrow Bye.
from Keith

4/22

Dear Keith,
E.S.L. is good I Like school.
I Like all the teacher's. Do you
Like school? who is yourfaviort
teacher? kcan you come to my
house?
see you tomareow
Diyar amin

7.16 *After learning to write in Kurdish, eleven year-old Keith translated his English entry into his buddy Diyar's native language.*

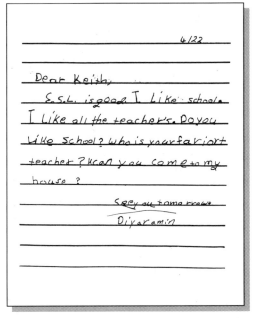

7.17 *Diyar's response shows careful letter formation in manuscript and use of standard spelling and punctuation.*

ESL Buddies

Sixth-grader Diyar was an eleven year-old Kurdish boy who had been in the U.S. less than three months and had gone to school in Iraq for only two years. Keith was an eleven year-old white student who had lived only in America. Their teacher, Mary Jo, thought buddy journals could benefit both students. In choosing to be journal buddies with Diyar, Keith said "I want to be friends with these kids. I want to help them learn to speak English. I feel sorry about what happened down in Iraq with Saddam Hussein killing them all. Some of their families died. If I were them I would like to know more language and American."

Keith was eager to befriend Diyar and said, "I showed Diyar how to write the ABC's in our language and how to do commas and periods and question marks. And he showed me how to write in his language." In one of his journal entries, Keith carefully translated his own English into Kurdish for Diyar, who was able to read it back to him. Diyar responded to Keith, even imitating Keith's spelling of "faviort" for "favorite" and included accurate punctuation for the most part. Diyar was also able to read his own entries orally (Figures 7.16 and 7.17). When asked who his friends were, Diyar listed his brothers, his sister, two other ESL students, and Keith, suggesting an important relationship with Keith.

As you can see from Keith and Diyar, when second-language learners are matched with English-speaking students for corre-

59

spondence in buddy journals, there are several advantages.

Buddy journals help combat the isolation many ESL students feel. This form of interactive writing may remove cultural and racial barriers between English-speaking and ESL students, as well (Foster, 1989). English-speaking students gain confidence and competence when they serve as language models and mentors for second-language learners who are beginning readers and writers. As well, second-language learners often teach their English-speaking buddies how to write and speak in their native language.

Whether ESL students speak and write little English or are well on their way to developing English literacy, buddy journals let them practice a range of written communication as their abilities allow. They can draw pictures and maps, label them with single words, and converse in phrases, sentences, or the longer format of a letter.

Peers encourage reading and writing about a broader range of topics and in different and sometimes more personal ways than journal dialoguing with teachers. Through buddy journals, students can establish positive relationships as they develop awareness, understanding, appreciation, and respect for other cultures.

Tips For Success

1. First, decide whether buddy journals will be a project within your own classroom or a collaborative venture where you team with another teacher and class, either at your own grade level or across grade levels. Both help build relationships since even students in the same class often do not have time in the regular day to get to know one another well. Cross-class buddies help build ties within a school and may even result in other types of inter-class collaborations related to curriculum.

2. To pair buddies, you might use random matching. Have half the children in the class put their names on slips of paper and the remaining students pull slips from a hat to determine who their buddies will be. You may need to discuss with children the chance element in a random draw and the implications for building positive self-esteem by graciously accepting a budddy one would not normally seek. Limiting the time for buddy journals to about two or three weeks also ensures that children's attitudes will be positive.

   Other ways of matching children include by free choice, by similarities or dissimilarities, by birthplace or birthdays, by interests, or by hair or eye color.

3. Describe buddy journals to students telling them what your objectives are. It is important that students understand the "why" of this interactive writing if they are to be committed.

   You may want to inform parents as well, so they understand that this informal, personal writing has an important place in your classroom writing program, both as a precursor and adjunct to academic writing. Among others, your objectives may be for students to:

   • Build fluency in reading and writing.

   • Build peer relationships and friendships.

Buddy Journals

1. Write about yourself.
2. Write about your hobbies
3. Write about your pets
4. Write about your interests, favorite things.
5. Ask questions
6. Write about problems / concerns
7. Give compliments
8. Write about adventures, vacations, school.
9. Write about your friends, weekend plans.
10. Write about a wish you have.

7.18 Sixth grade students generated this list of topics they could write about in their buddy journals.

6th Gr. Buddy Journals

1. Volunteers only. But once you commit you must continue for 3 wks.
2. 1st time → Choose name from hat (ESL → Volunteers)
   2nd time → You pick your buddy
3. Last 15 min. of Reading class to write.
   - If you don't participate, you read a book.
   - Ice cream social or pizza party during April test week.
4. Entries
   - Date
   - Greeting
   - Closing
   - Signature
5. Occasionally someone will read the journal.
   ! Nothing said in the journal that shouldn't be said in school.

7.19 These sixth grade students and their teacher created rules for writing in buddy journals.

- Establish understanding, appreciation and respect for other cultures.

4. To keep buddy conversations fresh, try these techniques:

   - periodically go back to solitary journal writing in which students write only for themselves

   - occasionally dialogue yourself with students in their journals;

   - change buddies so that students have opportunities to read and write about a range of topics with other children they do not know so well;

   - use buddy journals in content area classes such as science, social studies, or math for summarizing, reflecting, and processing information. Students can share new knowledge with each other or pose unanswered questions for peers to think about and answer.

   - suggest that students focus on student opinions of a current school, community, national, or international event that is supported with facts, evidence, and logical arguments.

5. Brainstorm a list of possible topics students can write about and rules for writing in buddy journals. Post on a bulletin board or put a copy in each journal. Keeping a list of ideas close at hand gives hesitant students ready access to topics they can explore. Posting writing rules reminds students of what is expected. Mary Jo's sixth-grade students

created the topics and rules in Figures 7.18 and 7.19 as they began to use buddy journals.

6. Teachers of younger children or ESL students who have little knowledge of English can have buddies make one journal together so there is only one conversation occurring between the two. For students with greater English proficiency, two simultaneous conversations may work.

7. Model the form and content of several entries yourself or write some with students using their input and suggestions. The overhead projector is an effective way to do this.

8. Allow at least 10 to 15 minutes for writing. Encourage drawing and labelling pictures with words or phrases, which is especially appropriate for students who are beginning to learn a language.

9. Younger students and those beginning to learn English do well when they are allowed to sit side-by-side for journal writing. In this way ESL students can receive verbal coaching from their buddies about spelling or punctuation as they write. Both students can read their entries orally to each other as well.

10. Establish and follow a regular monitoring schedule. For example, check journal entries weekly for the status of buddy relationships and for appropriate content.

11. Ask for volunteers to share interesting, funny, or well-written entries, as time allows. Reading journal entries to each other helps reinforce vocabulary and gives practice in oral reading, which is especially important for ESL students.

12. Build in some time for buddies to work or play together at a task or activity to strengthen the relationship and personalize the writing. Time to engage in face-to-face interactions such as collaborating on a science experiment or a social studies report creates real reasons to listen, talk, write, and read together. This practice also provides ESL students critical opportunities to work with English-speaking peers on meaningful tasks.

13. Evaluate after 2–3 weeks to rematch buddies if necessary or try another form of journals. Some teachers move back to personal journals or dialogue journals, or stop journal writing altogether for a time if buddy journals seem to be "losing steam."

References

Bromley, K. (1989). Buddy journals make the reading-writing connection. *The Reading Teacher*, *43*, 122–129.

Foster, L.A. (1989). Breaking down racial isolation. *Educational Leadership*, *47*, 76–77.

CHAPTER 8

Book Buddy Journal

Aimee is a third grade student who is a struggling reader and writer. Kristin is a university student in a master's program in education. The book buddy journal they shared linked a class of teachers taking a graduate course in reading with third graders receiving supportive instruction from their school's reading teacher.

The idea for book buddy journals originated with a reading teacher who suggested the school-university collaboration to a faculty member at a local university. A graduate student taking the course was invited to help implement the program.

Graduate students and their third-grade buddies corresponded weekly in journals structured around folktales they were both reading and webbing activities they both participated in. Why folktales? Folktales contain traditional story elements and are a popular genre of literature with children. As well, they contain fast-paced action, clearly delineated characters, and simple plots. They incorporated a webbing strategy because it involves active meaning-making through reading and writing. Students used the webs

to organize and integrate important information as they reconstructed the elements of stories (Bromley, 1991; Davis & McPherson, 1989).

Aimee's favorite part of her journal is two pages on which she and her buddy, Kristin, list the things they share. "We're both the oldest sisters in our family. We both have short hair. We like... earrings, reading chapter books, school and even homework, pizza, apples a lot, hamsters, dogs, wearing boots. . ." read the pages of the journal. The two might have added that they also learned a lot from the journal they kept together in which they conversed in writing as they got to know each other better, shared their responses to folktales, and used webbing to help identify the story elements of literature.

The purposes of the journals were: 1) to create enthusiasm and authentic reading and writing events for "at-risk" readers, 2) to allow teachers and children to share folktales and to use webbing to learn about story elements, 3) to allow everyone to experience the interactive nature of reading and writing and the role of audience in writing.

Implementing Book Buddies

Aimee was reading a year and a half below grade level, had never read an entire book herself, rarely completed her work in the classroom, and was negative about school. Brent was easily distracted, disliked reading and writing, was reading two years below grade level, lacked fluency as a writer, and rushed through his assignments, completing most inaccurately. These descriptions are typical of the other children in this group and may remind you of some of your own struggling readers.

Aimee's and her classmates' book buddy project began in September with each child choosing a buddy by pulling a name from a hat. Children used a plastic spiral binding machine to make journals from lined paper and tagboard. They personalized their journal covers with colored markers and collage art, and each journal held the correspondence between buddies. The children and adults spent 45 minutes a week for 10 weeks corresponding with each other. The graduate students carried the journals between the school and university and worked with the reading teacher to give children individual help.

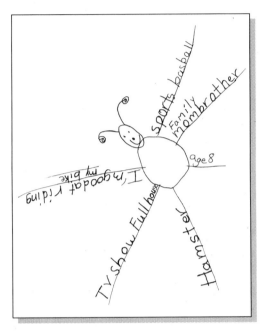

8.1 Aimee identifies important things about herself.

To prepare for the correspondence, the reading teacher modelled webbing as a prewriting strategy by first creating a web of personal information about her interests, hobbies, family, job, and so on, from which she then wrote a letter. Children then created their own webs and letters. The graduate students responded in a similar fashion, sending a videotape of messages to the children as well (see Figures 8.1–8.3). In turn, the children wrote back and sent photos to the adults. These initial entries established rapport and a comfortable context for interaction.

As the first four entries were exchanged, both children and adults learned how to web the elements of story. In subsequent journal exchanges, individuals in one group 1) chose

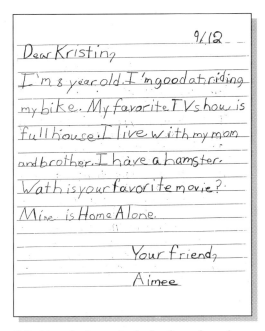

9/12

Dear Kristin,

I'm 8 year old. I'm good at riding my bike. My favorite TV show is full house. I live with my mom and brother. I have a hamster. Wath is your favorite movie? Mine is Home Alone.

Your friend,

Aimee

8.2 *Aimee's letter includes facts from her web to which she adds her favorite movie and a question.*

9/16

Dear Aimee,

Thank you for your letter! I'm glad we will be writing to each other. You have nice handwriting!

I am 20 years older than you, and I am still in school! I am studying how to become a teacher. Do you have any tips for me? I would really like some advice. I bet you could tell me some important things about what makes a good teacher.

I love movies, but I haven't seen Home Alone. I will have to rent it. My favorite movie is The Sound of Music. It's an old one! Have you seen it?

I like to ride bikes too. I have a mountain bike. I also play tennis and run. I love to ski in the winter when it is not too cold.

I am not married. Are you? ☺ I can't wait to hear from you again.

Sincerely,

Kristin

8.3 *Kristin responds to Aimee's letter of introduction with her own letter.*

a folktale for buddies to read; 2) read the folktale first themselves; 3) created webs to represent some of the folktale's story elements; and 4) invited their buddies to add missing elements.

Folktales and journals were then sent together to the other group. Webbing in the journals was like a dialogue. Buddies read the same story and contributed individual opinions about various story elements to create a complete web.

Children often met in small groups with either the reading teacher or graduate students to retell, discuss, and identify story elements of the folktales they were reading. At first, children could not easily identify problem, solution, and theme. Specific lessons, focused first on setting, characters,

and events, helped children understand problems and solutions. Lessons using brief fables helped children understand and verbalize theme.

Brent's Book Buddy Journal

The following entries show how Jan, one of the graduate students and a special education teacher, interacted with Brent to reinforce his knowledge of story elements. Jan learned from the journal that Brent liked animals, had several different pets at home, and played receiver in football. She knew, too, that modifications might make reading more interesting and easier for him. Jan used colored markers, calligraphy, drawings, and stickers to motivate her buddy. Parts of Jan's journal follow:

Since you like animals and have a little zoo at home, I picked out a folktale with animals for you. Big Talk has kangaroos as main characters. These animals live in Australia, but not here in America. There is a story web for Big Talk after this letter.

On the web you will put in the characters and the setting. Next to my idea of what I thought Big Talk's theme was, you will fill in what you think the theme was for the story. I am looking forward to what a special football player thinks these kangaroos are trying to tell us we should do in life. Looking forward to your next special letter!

In response, Brent added missing story elements, spelling "kangaroo" and "Australia" correctly, and identified his theme for the story (Figure 8.4). In his journal entry, he continued to tell Jan more about himself and answered her question "Is your cat, Midnight, black like a moonless sky?" He wrote, "My cat is black as the moon. My bird is blue as the sky." and told her that he collects football cards and is sometimes a quarterback.

In a later entry, Jan chose another folktale, tape recorded it, and sent it to Brent saying:

So, my defensive football player, let's tackle the story Tricky Tortoise and fill in the game plan (web). I filled in the players (characters) in the story. You have to list the plays (the events) that took place in

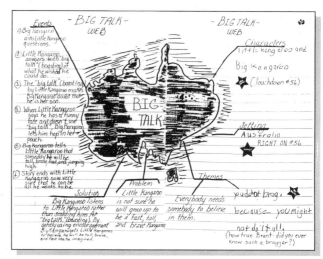

8.4 Jan creates a web for Big Talk and Brent adds his ideas.

the story, the problem, and the strategy to turn the story around (the solution). You also have to report on the web what the overall game plan of the story was (the theme). I already wrote my theme on the web. Just like two sportscasters reporting on a football game, each sportscaster will have his/her own theme (moral or main idea) about why the game went the way it did. So, write away Brent!

Brent accurately supplied the missing elements, spelling "elephant" and "tortoise" correctly, and wrote a letter to Jan. (Figure 8.5). He ended with, "I hope you do'nt mine the mistakes." Unasked, he also taped himself reading the story and sent it to Jan who wrote that she and her students listened to his tape as they followed the story. Brent chose *The Bremen Town Musicians* for Jan to read next and taped an oral reading for

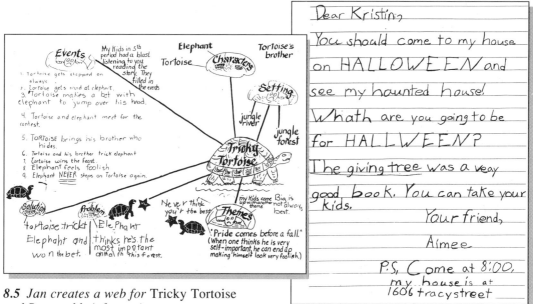

8.5 *Jan creates a web for* Tricky Tortoise *and Brent adds information.*

Dear Kristin,

You should come to my house on HALLOWEEN and see my haunted house! Whath are you going to be for HALLWEEN? The giving tree was a veay good book. You can take your kids.

Your friend,

Aimee

P.S. Come at 8:00, my house is at 1606 tracystreet

8.6 *The friendship between Aimee and Kristin grows.*

Dear Aimee,

You did a nice job in completing the web I made of The Giving Tree! I'm glad that you thought it was a good book too. I found that it took me a lot of thought to write down a theme, problem and resolution. Now it is your turn to figure out what these are in The Great Big Enormous Turnip. Good luck! (I know you can do it. ☺)

I would love to come to your Halloween Party! I am the world's biggest chicken though, and I am going to be very scared by your haunted house. Is your house in Endwell? I will try to find out and come. It sounds like fun. I will be dressing up as "Goofy" the dog. How about you? ✓

Your Friend,
Kristin

8.7 *Kristin's letter to Aimee shows their friendship's growth.*

her. They collaborated on webs to represent characters' traits for this book.

Brent, his classmates, and their buddies read several folktales and continued to collaborate on the webbing of story elements over the course of ten weeks. They created webs of descriptive words to represent characters and webs to compare folktales they had read. At the same time the buddies continued their correspondence through letters (Figures 8.6 and 8.7).

At the end of the ten weeks, the children invited their buddies to a pizza party in the school cafeteria where everyone talked, reread journals, shared pizza and juice, and exchanged addresses and telephone numbers. Meeting buddies face-to-face was a high point for everyone.

Evaluating the Project

The attitudes of Aimee and her classmates changed. They became excited and enthusiastic readers and writers. The graduate student who took the journals back and forth said "They (the children) would see me coming down the sidewalk and they practically fell out the door to get their hands on the journals." Weekly anecdotal notes kept by the reading teacher included comments that showed the children's eagerness to receive, read, and share their journals with each other. She often noted that before class the children reread previous entries and shared their journals with friends. As well, attitudes about reading, measured on a 20-item survey, increased significantly over the course of the 10 week project.

Looking at journal entries showed several things. First, the content of entries changed as friendships grew. The reading teacher noted initially that many children asked "What should I write?" and entries were tentative. But, after receiving the first letters from buddies, there were only occasional questions about spelling and none about content. For example, Doug had little trouble asking Lisa for her opinion about what a character might have done, giving his opinion, and telling Lisa about his plans to color his hair for Halloween.

Most entries were social in content, with children apt to write about their current interests and activities and graduate students following the children's lead. Many children used the journal to share life events like, "We have a new baby," as well as reveal problems such as, "I have a cousin. He goes to a special school because he fights with kids all the time." As they came to know the children, the adults were more open as well. For example, Jan revealed much about her own children and family life.

Some buddies, like Aimee and Kristen, met outside school. Many buddies continued their friendships through letter writing and meetings after the project ended. Three months later, Brent's mother said, "The books, gifts, cards, tapes, and letters have continued since the program ended!"

Second, special graphics in the journals helped focus attention and interest on reading and writing. The webs, coupled with pictures, appealed to the children. Many children imitated their buddies' uses of pictures, making drawings a part of their webs too. Specifically, the reading teacher, Brent's buddy, and Brent's mother noted his enthusiasm and commitment throughout the project. He eagerly reponded and imitated Jan's drawings and her use of colored pens and stickers. He could hardly wait to get his journal, read it, and write back to Jan, which was markedly different reading and writing behavior than he had exhibited previously.

Third, modelling and collaboration resulted in literacy learning. For example, children's understanding of story elements improved. At the end of the project, 17 children could use webs to accurately represent story elements, with solution and theme missed most often by three children. Additionally, children were asked to define setting, characters, plot, theme, problem, and solution. Their scores on the six items went from an average of 1 at the beginning to 5.5 at project end, demonstrating improvement in knowledge of story elements.

There were also changes in the reading

and writing behaviors of these children in their regular classrooms. Teachers commented on the children's excitement about the project and reported that they often shared their journals and folktales with other students. The children began to read during sustained silent reading time, something they had not done in the past. Children's writing improved with story elements more clearly included in their book reports.

When the children were asked what they liked most about book buddy journals they said:

The webs because you got to figure out the problem, the plot and all that stuff. It was fun.

Writing in the journals and sharing ideas.

Getting the letters back and seeing what they wrote.

I learned a lot more stuff about story elements and reading. That it's really, really, really fun.

I used to not read much and now I started reading chapter books.

The most unexpected things several children said they learned about writing, related to mechanics:

How to spell words. When I spelled one wrong she'd tell me how to spell it or I could look to see how she wrote it.

Where to put capitals and periods in better places.

Write slow so you don't make so many mistakes.

The graduate students found the first-hand experience with children personally rewarding. They learned that audience, purpose, and an opportunity to be creative in a non-threatening context are critical to children's enthusiasm about reading and writing.

Tips For Success

With a little creativity, you can adapt the book buddy project described here to make use of your available resources and to meet your students' needs. Some ideas follow:

1. Older elementary students, high school students, senior citizens or residents of nursing homes, and parents of your students may be eager to volunteer as book buddies and have much to share.

2. Students from across the community, state, or country might form a book club to read the work of a particular writer and share conversations with each other about the author's collected work.

3. Students from within one school or nearby schools might become book buddies who read books that complement the science or social studies curriculum.

4. Students might collaborate within the pages of their journals to write poetry, reports, essays, plays, or sequels based on books they read together.

5. If you decide to use folktales as a foundation for book buddy journals, you might ask students if they have favorites, check with your school media specialist for recommendations, or consult a literature anthology for ideas.

References

Bromley, K.D. (1991). *Webbing With Literature: Creating Storymaps With Children's Books.* Boston: Allyn & Bacon.

Davis, Z.T., & McPherson, M.D. (1989). Story map instruction: A road map for reading comprehension. *The Reading Teacher, 43,* 232–240.

To Learn More

Bromley, K., Winters, D., & Schlimmer, K. (1994). Book Buddies: Creating Enthusiasm for Literacy Learning. *The Reading Teacher, 47,* 1.

CHAPTER 9

Double Entry Journal

Thinking is a dialogue we have with ourselves. . . a continuing effort to review the meanings we are making in order to see further what they mean.

This quote from *The Journal Book* by Ann Berthoff (Heinemann, 1987) describes the essence of the dialectical notebook or double entry journal. A double entry journal is one in which students keep two separate entries related to the same topic, idea, or activity. Pages in a spiral-bound notebook or sheets in a handmade journal can become double entry pages by drawing a line down the middle of each page from top to bottom to create two columns. Students write their first entries, which are reports of information, summaries of events, objective accounts of something, quotations, or sketches in the left-hand column. In the right-hand column, directly opposite these entries, they make their second entries—personal observations, feelings about or a rehashing of the

topic, or interpretations of the factual entries in their first columns.

The double entry journal is a tool for thinking. Ann Berthoff reminds us that it ". . .makes the powerful instrument of analogy available to writers as a way of looking and looking again. . ." She says that when the writer says something, looks at it, thinks about it, and then writes an associated thought, this is a first step in thinking in analogies. She adds that "practice in double entry journals is practice in analogizing and thus practice in critical and creative thought."

Advantages

Double entry journals have several advantages for students at all grade levels who have at least beginning skills in writing. One advantage of the double entry journal is that it encourages students to make connections between their own knowledge and information that is new to them. According to learning theory, this link between the new and known is vital in order for understanding and learning to take place.

A second advantage of the double entry journal is the opportunity it gives students to rethink and reassess an idea or new information. Thinking occurs when one looks at something again, asks a question, and considers alternatives. These mental activities are the very nature of what happens in a double entry journal. When your students look and look again at what they have written, they are poised to interpret and analyze. Their double entry journals also serve as a rich storehouse of analogies to use as examples in their writing or as topics for compositions. Of course, your students may need help seeing the value of the analogous statements they have written. When you teach a mini-lesson using your students' journals, aimed specifically at developing analogies, they will be most successful with it.

A third advantage of this type of journal is the links it establishes among reading, writing, listening, speaking, and thinking. Double entry journals have a variety of uses in the classroom that reinforce all the modes of communication. Double entry journals can serve as a place to link listening and writing as your students take notes from a lecture, movie, or video. In double entry journals, your students link writing and speaking when they share entries orally with each other. When your students take notes as they read stories or textbooks, they establish links between reading and writing. Then, as your students revisit their notes to paraphrase, extend, comment on, question, interpret, and analyze the words they have written, the critical link with thinking is reinforced.

"Book and Me" Entries

Kisten, a fifth grade teacher, read *Number The Stars* by Lois Lowry (Houghton Mifflin, 1989) to her class as part of a study of war and peace. She read a chapter a day and asked her students to keep double entry journals related to the story. The headings they used were "Book " and "Me." After hearing a chapter, students entered short summaries of what the chapter was about on the left side of the page. On the right side they described what the chapter reminded them of in their own lives or how it made them feel.

Justin, a struggling reader and writer, shows in his entries (Figure 9.1) that he was beginning to see parallels between a story and his own life. He compared the opening of a casket to a similar scene in "Dracula" that he had watched on TV. He also linked Ann Marie's discovery of her mother to his finding a helpless squirrel. Kisten encouraged her students to make these kinds of connections to their everyday lives because she believed that this type of analogy-making is an important key to understanding.

Maryann, a resource room teacher of 6th, 7th, and 8th grade students with learning disabilities and emotional and mental handicaps, also found double entry journals useful. She read a chapter a day to her students from *Tuck Everlasting* by Natalie Babbitt (Farrar, Straus & Giroux, 1975) and had them keep double-sided journals (Figure

9.1 *A page from Justin's double entry journal showing his response to Chapters 9–12 of* Number The Stars *by Lois Lowry.*

9.2 *A page from Rob's double entry journal showing his response to* Tuck Everlasting *by Natalie Babbitt.*

9.2). They also used the headings "Book" and "Me." Maryann asked them to date each entry as well. To build comprehension, she had students relate in some way to what they heard in the "Me" column, either telling what it reminded them of or making a prediction about what they thought might happen next. After listening to Chapter 10, Rob made a prediction about what might happen next, evidence that he was involved in the story and understood what he heard.

Tips For Success

Both Kisten and Maryann found that after a time, interest in the journals began to wane for some of their students. They responded by regularly reading journal entries to legiti-

mize the activity, to see what the students were writing, to ensure that they were thinking about what they heard, and to get them back on track if need be. Other techniques for keeping interest high include:

1. Write messages to children in their journals. You can see the kinds of comments and questions Kisten and Maryann made to Justin and Rob in Figures 9.1 and 9.2. In their dialogues with students these teachers supported, reinforced, questioned, and nudged a bit, and they found that interest picked up. Kisten and Maryann learned that when students know their journals will be read by someone and occasionally find a note written to them, there is not only a difference in student commitment to writing in the

journals, but also a difference in what they write.

2. Look to literature and beyond to supply the "stuff" of students' journals.

In math: Use double entry journals to help students see solutions more clearly and then visualize the process for solving problems. For students who are not yet fluent writers, you can suggest they sketch pictures or draw diagrams and label them as an aid to understanding problems.

In science: The format of the double entry journal lends itself well to the development of skills in observation and problem solving in science. When your students use one column or page to describe what they observe during a science experiment, they can use the other column or page to question and hypothesize about their observations.

In listening and reading: As your students hear lectures or read content area textbooks, writing twice about information or ideas, once to record and once to process and personalize what they have first written, gives them opportunities to ponder, reflect, and perhaps form opinions.

3. Use double entry journals to recognize ESL students' native languages and to reinforce their acquisition of English. Have ESL students write in their native language in one column while a buddy translates on the other (or vice versa).

4. Try a triple entry journal. Have students make three columns using the length of a notebook page and label them "Book," "Me," "World." Under "Book," students quote or paraphrase from material they read, under "Me" they relate their own experiences, and under "World" they relate both of those entries to the world in general.

References

Berthoff, A.E. (1987). Dialectical Notebooks and the Audit of Meaning. In Toby Fulwiler (Ed.) *The Journal Book*, Portsmouth, NH: Heinemann (pp. 11–18).

CHAPTER 10

Draw and Tell Journal

Kara's kindergarten class looked like a five-year-old version of the United Nations. Among her young students were Chinese, Korean, Russian, Italian, and African-American children, as well as children with Eastern European backgrounds. Some of her students were aware of differences in classmates' skin, hair color, and languages spoken at home, although everyone spoke English at school.

Kara wanted to create an environment in her classroom to celebrate this diversity. She wanted her children to be proud of their individual heritages and to learn more about each other. Kara also wanted to develop the oral language skills of some of her children who were not yet talking easily with each other or her. She wanted to introduce books to a few children who were not read to at home. And she wanted to try an experiment with journals in kindergarten.

Kara found that the folktale-based "draw and tell" journal was a way to accomplish these goals. Kara found a folktale to represent the culture or country of each of her students. She decided on folktales not only for the direct connection to her children's backgrounds, but also because they are usu-

ally brief, fast-paced stories that contain easily identified characters. She decided to read a folktale to her class twice a week. To develop students' literacy skills and further their understandings about the different cultures, Kara planned to follow up each reading with related interactive activities, to have children to draw pictures about the stories, and to invite them to talk with their classmates about those pictures.

To give children a place to record stories they heard and to hold their drawings, Kara helped them make "draw and tell" journals. She believed that these journals could provide her with information about her children's literacy development and would be a good record of some of the class's activities to send home to parents as well. Each journal had a colored construction paper cover and was made of several sheets of white art paper. Kara punched holes and used yarn to tie the journals together. Children drew pictures of themselves on the covers where Kara also printed their names in large letters. Kara added a list of folktales and authors to each student's journal.

Listen, Draw, and Tell

Ready for their first journal experience, Kara's students gathered on a rug to listen to the folktale. To help children develop reference points for each story, Kara posted a world map in the classroom. Each time she read a story, children marked the place on the map where that story came from. They used pieces of yarn to connect the countries of the folktales' origins with their present location.

After listening to the story, talking about it, and rereading the story at her students' request, Kara modelled for the children how to "draw and tell." In her own journal, she drew a picture, put a caption on it, and then told the class about it. Following this, children returned to circular tables where they sat in small groups as they drew in their journals. Kara kept crayons, magic markers, and journals in an open cupboard so they were easily accessible to the children. Most children could find their own journal by its cover with their picture and name.

At first, as they drew in their journals, Kara sat with the children and drew in her own journal. Then she moved quietly among them talking with individual children about their pictures. Kara often asked "What did you draw?" or "Can you tell me about your

picture?" or "What is this?" She then used a marker to write children's responses on their pictures. Each time Kara transcribed what a child said, she read the child's words back, pointing to each word as she read, often having the child read with her. Drawing in the journals usually occurred after lots of group interaction and participation, including dramatizing parts of stories or retelling confusing parts using puppets.

As children drew their pictures, Kara observed them in conversations with each other, often naming the things they drew, requesting crayons of a certain color from each other, and telling about the actions depicted in their illustrations. Kara noticed that shy children who usually said little or nothing at group time, talked as they drew. After only a few folktales were read and pictures shared, all the children asked to tell the class about their pictures. Kara discovered that her students often had elaborate stories to tell, many going well beyond what they had drawn.

What Children Draw

Sometimes, Kara asked children to draw pictures of their favorite characters. Ben, for example, drew a picture of the wolf in response to the German version of *Little Red Riding Hood* by H. Pincus (Harcourt, 1968) and dictated two sentences for Kara to write (Figure 10.1). When he told his classmates about the picture, he told them the wolf was his favorite character because he was a "scary" wolf with big teeth, sharp claws, and big eyes. Ben pointed to these characteristics in his picture as he talked and reminded children of how the wolf looked in the

10.1 Ben drew the wolf, his favorite character from Little Red Riding Hood.

This is my favorite Character. This is the wolf.

The opening branches in the woods

10.2 Amy drew tree branches as hands that opened and closed to let the young girl and her grandmother through the forest.

Grandmother's nightcap. Describing characters' traits often prompted the telling of favorite parts of the story as well.

Other times Kara directed children to listen for something specific in the story, as when she read *The Talking Eggs,* a Creole tale from the American South by R. San Soucci (Scholastic, 1989). She asked them to listen for all the strange things that happened in that tale. After hearing the story, the children listed such things as bunnies dancing, a cow with two heads, eggs that talked, a bone that became stew, a piece of rice that turned into lots of rice, and woods that opened and closed. Kara then invited children to draw their favorite strange things that happened in the story. Amy drew a picture of the young girl and grandmother

(Figure 10.2) and dictated "The opening branches in the woods." When Amy told about the story, she described how the branches opened before them and closed after them as they walked through the forest.

Often children drew pictures of whatever they chose. After hearing the Japanese story, *Dawn* by M. Bang (Morrow, 1983), Kayleigh drew two figures in a hammock (Figure 10.3) and dictated to Kara "This is Dawn. She tries to find her mother and the Easter egg fell from the sky." She included her own scribbled lines on the left side of the picture, making her journal look like a page from the book Kara had read. In her drawing, Kayleigh demonstrates an awareness of this folktale's storybook format and of the way print is often arranged in rows beside

10.3 *Kayleigh made her picture look like a page from* Dawn, *and copied her name backwards with letters in reverse order.*

10.4 *Paul may have seen Strega Nona as a witch-character or he just wanted to draw a Halloween picture.*

illustrations. When she told her classmates about the picture, she described the characters in *Dawn* and extended the tale to include the humorous occurrence of eggs falling from the sky. Her story did not include an explanation of the text-like scribbles until Kara asked about them and then she said "That was a story."

Going Further

Kara often found that children finished drawing their pictures before she could conference with each one to write down what they wanted to say. One day, wondering what they had drawn and wanting to give them feedback on their journals, Kara took time while her students were in gym to look at

their pictures and wrote brief messages on stick-on notes to some of the children. These notes were greeted with such enthusiasm that she continued to use them to respond to drawing and telling activities. After hearing *Strega Nona* an Italian folktale by Tomie de Paola (Scholastic, 1975), Paul drew a picture of a ghost and witch (Figure 10.4). When Kara ran out of time for him to dictate a sentence about what he drew, she wrote a note in the upper right corner instead.

Sometimes Kara wrote statements and other times she asked questions in these notes. She quickly found that children were eager to have her read what she had written, but their responses to the questions was an unexpected surprise—children couldn't wait until journal sharing time to answer her questions. They wanted Kara to read each question to the group or they "read" it themselves and gave their answers. With further comments and questions from Kara, dialogues often resulted in which children revealed much to her, beyond what was evident in their pictures, about their understanding or misunderstanding of the folktale.

On the day Kara read *Lon Po Po*, the Chinese version of "Little Red Riding Hood" by E. Young (Scholastic, 1989) she prepared a journal page with lines and print (Figure 10.5), believing that some of the children were ready to do their own writing. After reading and talking about the story, Kara showed children a completed journal page on which she printed the title, *Lon Po Po*, and the name of her favorite character, Shang, as an example of what she wanted the children to do. She also showed them a drawing she had done of her favorite scene from the story. She found that many children copied her character and scene, so the next time she did this she asked the children to draw pictures that were different from her's.

Kara was pleased with her experiment with journals in kindergarten. She found the folktales an appropriate way to develop her children's awareness and appreciation of differences and similarities in each other's backgrounds. She found the journals a good vehicle for connecting reading with drawing, and for building her children's confidence and competence in oral language production. Kara also saw her children discover the connection between speech and print in their Draw-and-Tell Journals as they began to experiment with writing.

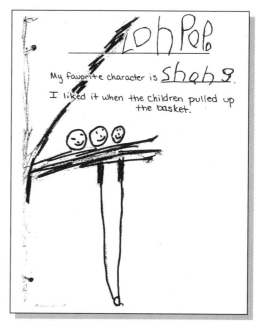

10.5 This child wrote the name of the story and her favorite character and drew the three children in the Ginko tree as they tricked the wolf.

Tips For Success

1. Kara's biggest concern with the Draw-and-Tell Journals was time. It was difficult to have time to get to conference with all the children and write down what they had to say about their pictures. You can address this problem by:

   • beginning the sharing process while some children finish their drawings instead of waiting until everyone finishes;

   • using stick-on notes to communicate with children if you haven't had a chance to let them tell you about their pictures and you are not sure what they have drawn. This works well when you run out of time and children will respond eagerly to them.

2. Another concern Kara had was that the journals were not made strongly enough and did not hold up. Some children asked to take their journals home to show their families and with all the use the journals had in the classroom, they did not hold up well. Construction paper covers tore easily and were not durable. Yarn came untied and didn't allow for pages to turn easily.

You can extend the life of your students' journals by using tagboard covers and metal rings. Contact paper covers, laminated covers, or clear plastic pocket folders also hold up to wear and moisture.

Home-School Journal

Rebecca,
I really like the picture you drew of yourself.
You are quite an artist. I love you.

Mommy

Rebecca,
Nice job on the picture of our family. I see you like to use purple. I know that is your favorite color. I love you.
Love
Mommy Melissa & Ryan

Rebecca,
You did a great job on our house. I really like the windows. You are very imaginative. Have a good week.
Love
Mommy

Teacher,
I think this is wonderful and I would be curious to hear of your observations of her skills and understanding. (Not necessarily every time).
Nancy T. (parent)

Dear Teacher,
This tells me a lot, that david's telling white fibs. We don't have a dog or farm animals or fish, or a father who lives here. I know a lot of this is normial.
Lousie W. (parent)

Dear Teacher,
David's been doing the dance's & songs at home, I'm glad to see he's finely sing & dancing.
Louise W.

Teacher,
Tyler seems very interested in this book even though he does not like coming to school. Very good idea, maybe Tyler will show more interest in school.
Debbie R. (parent)

I think this is a excelent idea, & a great way to get her started doing things w/others.

John N.

These excerpts from four students' Go-Home journals show how parents responded to their children's work. Rebecca, David, Tyler, and Heather were enrolled in a Head Start program. Their teacher, Debbie, wanted to build literacy skills and foster communication between parents and herself and also between parents and children. When Debbie introduced the journal to her students, she told them that they would each draw and write in their own journal and then take it home to show their parents who would also write back to them in it. So, parents were the audience for the children's journals and Debbie had created a natural vehicle for parent contact with her.

The journal was an easy way to inform parents about the activities going on in school, as well (Figures 11.1–11.4). For example, she used the journal as part of her "I Have A Friend" unit in which children learned about similarities and differences between themselves and others. The journals kept parents up to date on the unit so they could reinforce and extend learning at home.

Each week children drew pictures in their journals and Debbie included a letter to the parents about what was happening in school. In the first letter home, which she copied for each child and pasted into their journal, Debbie encouraged parents to write back to both the child and her (Figure 11.1). Children took their journals home every Thursday so they could share them with their families over the weekend, and brought

Dear

For the next several weeks our theme will be "I Have a Friend." Throughout the unit we will be exploring the similarities and differences among us. We hope our students will learn to celebrate these differences and become a classroom of friends.

This week we are looking at our physical characteristics such as hair and eye color. We made a chart of these traits to encourage pre-math skills. We are also exploring what our bodies can do. We traced our hands and named what we could do with them. We also learned the song "Head, Shoulders, knees and Toes." We made a face collage out of pictures that we cut out of magazines. We listened to the books We Are All the Same, We Are All Different and Black Is Brown Is Tan.

Finally, we started a go-home journal. The purpose of a go-home journal is to expand our writing skills. The first page is our letter to you. The next page is your child's entry. This week they made self-portraits. We encourage you to talk about these pictures with your child. A blank page is also included for your response. You may write to your child and/or us. Every Thursday these journals will be sent home with your child. Please return them (with your response) on Monday. Please leave all the pages in the journal. We are encouraging our students to create a book.

Thank you for your cooperation. We look forward to reading your responses. Feel free to ask us questions.

Sincerely,
Your Head Start teachers
Melonie, Jean, Penny, & Debbie

11.1

11.1–11.4 *Letters sent to parents of Head Start children by the teacher and aides.*

11.2

Dear

Thank you for your wonderful responses to last week's journal. Please keep writing.

This week we continued to focus on our physical differences and similarities. We set up a plexiglass window and paired the children up on either side of it. They each used fingerpaint to paint a picture of their friend on the plexiglass. We listened to the books I Have a Sister, My Sister Is Deaf, Arnie and the New Kid, and Where's Chimpy? We learned a new song called "Johnny Has One Hammer." We also did movement to music. For a journal entry this week, they asked their friend what they liked to play with and then drew a picture of their friend. We also made a banner with all of our hand prints on it.

As an added bonus, some firefighters from the local fire department visited us on Monday. They taught us to stop, drop, and roll if we ever catch on fire. They also talked about their job and showed us their uniforms and fire engines.

Next week we will be talking about our families. We would appreciate it if you could send a picture of your family in with your child so they can share it with the class. The pictures will be returned.

We look forward to hearing from you.

Sincerely,
Melonie, Jean, Penny, & Debbie

Dear
Thank you again for your responses. Your child loves to show us what you have written and every Thursday they are excited to bring their journal home to show you.

This week we talked about our families. We talked about the photographs you sent in, drew pictures of our families in our journals, and made pictures of our families using pipe cleaners and stencils at the art table. We read the books New Baby by McCully and Abiyoyo by Pete Seeger.

Since Halloween is coming we also went outside and filled a giant pumpkin bag with leaves. We also made spider hats and paper bag pumpkins.

Today we visited the Cider Mill. We saw how donuts and cider are made. The apple press was very noisy. As a special treat they gave us each a donut and a glass of cider. We had a lot of fun.

Sincerely,
Melonie, Jean, Penny, & Debbie

11.3

11.4

Dear
Thank you once again for your wonderful responses. Please remember to send this journal back to school on Monday with your child.

This week we are continuing our focus on families. We are looking at the cultural differences and similarities between families. We have had small group discussions about several different types of cultures using a flannel board. We read the books Boat Ride With Lillian Two Blossom and Babushka's Doll, both by Patricia Polacco. In our journals we drew pictures of our homes. We learned several new dances—Mexican hat dance, Hawaiian dance, and going on a walrus hunt. For art we made leis, sombreros, dolls, and walruses.

Sincerely,
Melonie, Jean, Penny, & Debbie

them back on Monday.

Journals were created from construction paper covers that held sheets of colored art paper stapled in prearranged order. The teacher's page was always yellow, the child's page was blue, and the parents' page was green. This gave some order to the journal and reinforced children's identification of these colors.

Just as Kara did in her Draw-and-Tell journals (see Chapter 10), Debbie asked children to tell her about their finished pictures. She often wrote what they said on their pictures, as well. For the first assignment, a self-portrait, Debbie had mixed responses. Jason drew himself with very long legs, traced his hand, and told Debbie all about his picture. Jessica scribbled on her page and wouldn't talk about her picture. Heather drew a turtle. Tyler scribbled all over the page and then said "I made a whole bunch of hair all over me." Debbie accepted what children did and noted their progress in later journal pictures.

Some teachers hold mini-conferences with each child on Friday before the journals go home (Ramsaur, 1992). In these meetings, you can read your comments to a child's parents and ask if there is anything else the child wants to add to the letter. This ensures that children know what their journals say and can perhaps even read parts of the letters to their parents.

The biggest disappointment in using home-school journals can be the lack of response from parents. About half of Debbie's parents wrote back in the journals the first time. That Monday she sent a note home with children who did not have their journals, asking for journals to be returned so more pages could be added. The note

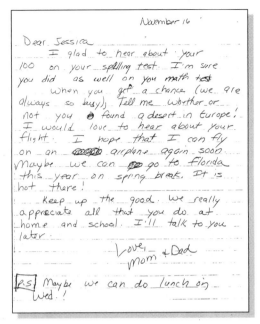

November 16

Dear Jessica

    I glad to hear about your 100 on your spelling test. I'm sure you did as well on you math test
    When you get a chance (we are always so busy) tell me whether or not you found a desert in Europe! I would love to hear about your flight. I hope that I can fly on an airplane again soon. Maybe we can go to Florida this year on spring break. It is hot there!
    Keep up the good. We really appreciate all that you do at home and school. I'll talk to you later.

Love,
Mom + Dad

P.S. Maybe we can do lunch on Wed.!

11.5 An entry in Jessica's Letter Home Journal written by her mother.

Dear Mom and Dad,
    In math we played Jeopardy. My group is in second place. Group six is in first. Me, Meridith, Brian and Justin are in group three. You should know all of them. We did lots of papers too.
    I use to always get one wrong on the spelling test. Now I get them all right, every time. I am writing a story. a long story. Meridith and me are writing a story but she typing it.
    We read all about the desert. We did a web about the desert. Then we answered questions about the desert.
    Last week we had a pizza party. But we wrote first. We had it because we got all 40 stars. School is cool! Write back soon.

Love
Jessica

11.6 An entry written by Jessica in her Letter Home Journal.

worked and the rest of the journals came back. Each week she had to send home three or four reminders.

Some journals came back without anything written by parents. Debbie wondered if some parents could not read, were not interested, or didn't understand the purpose of the journals. Two ideas may help solve this problem. Perhaps, inviting brothers, sisters, grandparents, or caregivers to respond, as well as parents, would ensure a written message in every child's journal. Also, explaining the purpose of the home-school journal at a parent-teacher conference early in the year promotes participation.

Debbie saw enthusiastic reactions from both children and parents to the drawing and writing in the journals. She observed chil-

dren eager to carry their journals back and forth between home and school. After a few weeks, Jason was starting to write his own name, and Tyler drew people and houses. Several parents commented that they liked knowing what went on in school and many praised and encouraged their children and their work in the journals.

Letter-Home Journals

Gregg, a third grade teacher, used a type of journal similar to Debbie's. He used "Letter-Home Journals" as a way for his students to record and reflect on their learning in science and social studies and to communicate with their parents. Like Debbie, he wanted to inform parents about what was happening in school and involve them more actively in their child's education.

Gregg introduced the journals as end-of-week letters to parents, telling his students he would read them and so would their parents, who were encouraged to write back. Gregg's students wrote their letters on Fridays in spiral notebooks that they used as journals. Like Debbie, Gregg was troubled by the fact that not all parents participated consistently and one never wrote back. From this lack of response, Gregg might learn that some parents do not have time, cannot write, or do not read or write English, all helpful pieces of information for trying to find effective ways to involve parents.

Jessica's entries told Gregg what she liked and didn't like about school, what she was learning, and how she was able to communicate in writing to her family (Figures 11.6 and 11.7). Both Jessica's parents responded regularly in her journal (Figures 11.5 and 11.8). In Jessica's case, she not only wrote about what she was doing in school, but often reminded her parents, as was the case with a science experiment about papermaking she had done in school, to "Ask me about it." Her father was clearly interested and wrote in a later entry "You can tell me tonight about your experiment on leaves." For Jessica, journal entries provided a way to summarize learning and they initiated conversations at home about school learning. Her parents' responses provided Jessica with tangible evidence of their interest and support.

11.7 The desert web Jessica drew to accompany her entry.

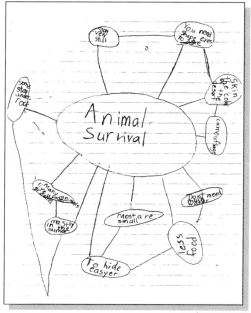

11.8 An entry in Jessica's Letter Home Journal written by her father.

> Nov. 23
>
> Dear Jessica,
>   It sounds like school is going pretty good for you. I am glad that your math is doing well. This will be a short week at school. It will be a short week for me at work also.
>   The section on deserts sounds interesting. Deserts are supposed to be beautiful but eerie places. I would like to spend some time in a desert.
>   I hope you have a good day at school! See you tonight.
>
>   Love,
>   Mom and
>   Dad.

While Gregg did not write entries in these Letter-Home Journals, perhaps because of a lack of time, he might have. Some teachers who use home-school journals write letters in 4 or 5 journals each week, and in a month's time they have written a letter to every family. Or, Gregg could make copies of a letter to parents and staple or glue it into each child's journal, as Debbie did. A personal letter to parents, written occasionally by you in the journal, confirms the journal's importance for both students and parents and gives you a direct line of communication to families.

Both Go-Home Journals and Letter-Home Journals create vehicles for students to explore drawing, writing, talking, and learning, and provide you with a record of their literacy growth. Through these journals, you can keep parents informed about school activities, as well. For many of your children, this type of journal will provide you with a window on the support structure for learning that is in place at home.

Tips For Success

If you are looking for a way to have better communication with parents, here are a few practical ideas for getting started and having success with journals that link home and school:

1. In September (or whenever you begin using the journals), send journals home with a letter to parents introducing yourself. End your letter with an invitation to parents to tell you about themselves. In future letters you can tell parents about the curriculum, homework, a project or something specific they might praise their child for.

2. Choose a special child each week and read the parent's entry to the entire class. This does wonderful things for a student's self-esteem and lets your students and parents know how much you value their letters.

3. Ask parents of beginning readers to read the entries they write to their children. As children learn to read, parents can encourage them to read the entries themselves. This provides a shared reading opportunity for parents and child and reading practice for the child.

4. Invite parents to write in journals about special family happenings. You will learn much about your children's lives and you can collect and publish these family stories in a class book of family histories (Shockley, 1993).

5. Give your students plastic recloseable bags to carry their journals back and forth between home and school. Journals will stay dry, clean, and in one piece longer.

References

Ramsaur, M.C. (1992). From teacher to parent to child. *Teaching K–8.* August/September, 78–84.

Shockley, B. (1993). Extending the literate community: Reading and writing with families. *The New Advocate, 6,* 1, 11–24.

CHAPTER 12

Character Journal

A character journal is a written diary kept by a reader as he or she assumes the role of the main character as a book is read.   (Hancock, 1993).

It is a place in which a writer adopts the personality of a story character and writes about the life of that character. A character journal provides opportunities for taking a different point of view or perspective, something we know is important for comprehension, problem solving, and learning in general. In this type of journal, a student becomes a character, experiencing the events and emotions of the character's life. Writing in a character journal requires using the author's vocabulary and language to document the story the way a character might.

Just as with many of the other journals described in this book, the character journal serves as raw material for later writing. It is a bridge, connecting your students to the more formal writing they do in school. The character journal functions in several ways:

Kim, a fourth grade teacher, read a chapter or two a day to her class from *Dear Mr. Henshaw* by Beverly Cleary (Morrow, 1983).

> The character journal enables students to take another's point of view and live life through a character's eyes.

Kim asked her students to pretend they were Leigh Botts and to keep a journal as he might. She gave them 10 or 15 minutes following her oral reading each day to make entries. In Kristen's March 26th entry (Figure 12.1), her writing shows how she has taken Leigh's point of view. She thinks like Leigh and offers a solution about who the lunchbox thief is. In her March 27th entry, she describes Leigh's elation at the prospect of his mother and father getting back to-

March 25

After dinner after Barry left, I asked mom if there was a chance that she would get married to dad again. She said no because all he cared about was his truck and also she never knew where he was. That was the end of that conversation. The next day at school my alarm didn't go off but I wasn't surprised. I decided that I would keep the alarm for one more day.

March 26

About 2 hours after I went to sleep I was awaken by the sound of my alarm! I opened my eyes and I was in front of my refrigerator eating the good things out of my lunch. Then my mother came in and said "WHAT ON EARTH IS GOING ON DOWN HERE?" I told my mother what happened. I finally knew who the theif was.

Good use of quotation   *Clever!*

March 27

Right before I went to bed I heard a truck in the driveway. I looked out my window and saw my dad and "BANDIT" I exlaimed. Mom told me to go up in my room while she talked to dad. I tried to hear what they were saying. This is all I heard: "Please Bonnie. I'll even quit my job and get another one." That was dad. A couple of minutes later I heard footsteps coming up the stairs. Mom and dad came in. Mom said "Leigh. I have something I want to tell you." Then dad interrupted and said. "We are going to get married again." I was so happy I started jumping up and down as though I was crazy. I went over and hugged Bandit and said to myself "We're going to be one big happy family again."

Good comparison!
I can feel your excitement!!

March 28

That morning when I went to school I had just remembered that I forgot to write a story for the Young Writers Yearbook! So right when I got in my classroom I started writing it. It was called A Day with Dad. It was about the time I rode with dad in his trucks.

March 29

When I went to school that morning everybody was going to find out who won the book contest. When I opened up the year book I had won first place!! I was so excited. And guess who the mystery auther was? Mr. Henshaw!! About 2 days later I met Mr. Henshaw. my life has changed alot. I'm especially glad that dad moved in with us.

How has it changed?

September

Weell, today is my first day of 7th grade. I'm sorry I got so far behind in my diary. I have tons of friends now. Now I know I'm not so medium. This is going to be my last entry in my diary. Well, bye.

I love how you used the phrase Leigh used at the beginning of the book.

Sincerely,

Leigh Botts

Kristin,
You really adopted the role of Leigh! It was easy to believe that you were Leigh. I especially like your idea that you were the lunchbox thief. Wonderful job!!

12.1 Kristen, a fourth grader, takes the point of view of Leigh Botts in her character journal.

gether again. In the March 29th entry, she makes a retrospective statement noting how much her (Leigh's) life has changed since meeting Mr. Henshaw. In this journal, Kristen adopted Leigh's personality and viewed the events of the story from his perspective.

The emotions characters feel and the events in their lives are perhaps more poignantly felt by your students when they become those characters and write as the characters would. When you ask your students to take someone else's perspective, you ask them to think differently than they ordinarily might. This kind of thinking can be mind-expanding. It not only enhances comprehension and problem-solving, but learning in general.

> The character journal develops content area knowledge and understanding across the curriculum.

Nancy's fifth-grade class was studying Westward Expansion. To support what her students were reading in their content area text, Nancy chose to read *Sacagawea*, by B. Skold (Dillon, 1977). She felt this biography of the Indian woman who assisted Lewis and Clark on their expedition up the Missouri River into the northwest territories in the 1894 would be more interesting to them since it was a real person's experience.

To further engage her students, Nancy asked them each to choose one of the characters and "become" that person in the journal. She made no rules about correct spelling and gave no grades. Her students kept these journals only as a way to get to know history through a real person's eyes and to practice writing.

Daniel became Sacagawea in his character journal (Figure 12.2). In his entries, Daniel shows how he put himself in her place as he lived through the feelings and experiences she had on her journey. He shows that he understands Sacagawea's role and her feelings, and that he has some knowledge of the geography and terrain the expedition covered. He also demonstrates his content area knowledge by using appropriate social studies vocabulary, for example, Toussaint Charbonneau, Jean Baptiste, Captain Lewis, Platte River, Rocky Mts., Columbia River, salmon, and Pacific Ocean. Notice also Daniel's correct spelling of these content area terms.

As you can see, this type of journal writing allows your students to paraphrase and document their content area knowledge. Writing as a character might write reinforces the understanding of social studies concepts. It also has a positive effect on spelling as your students use content area vocabulary.

The aesthetic response a reader has to print forms the basis for understanding that print (Rosenblatt, 1985). You read about this emotional experience or transaction with print in Chapter 4. The character journal helps students have

> The character journal enriches the reading experience and helps students appreciate a wide range of literature.

12.2 In this character journal, Daniel, a fifth grader, becomes Sacagawea.

aesthetic responses. It helps them "get into" literature and is an especially good way to bring print to life for struggling readers. Poor readers and students who don't like reading often see books as full of print to decipher and decode, not filled with people to meet and places to visit. But, when students read or listen to a story from the perspective of one of the characters, they build empathy for that character and have deeper, richer encounters with the print that tells the character's story.

For many younger as well as older students, the genres of biography and historical fiction are not popular. There are a number of reasons for this. Perhaps it is because our culture seems to value the present more than it does the past. Or, perhaps it is because these stories are often set in times gone by and in places that are not familiar to students. Sometimes the dialogue and vocabulary of biography and historical fiction seem unrealistic and difficult to relate to. Whatever the reasons, it can be a challenge to interest students in these genres.

Character journals provide a way to make the past and people's lives come to life. In the character journal, your students can enter into life as others have known it and as it is depicted in literature. Through writing they can experience the conflicts, disappointments, satisfactions, hopes, and dreams of other people.

> The character journal can be a bridge, connecting students to more formal writing.

Writing in a character journal that is not graded or evaluated helps build your students' fluency. If the journal is a risk-free place to write, then your students can feel comfortable as they try out new words while they explore and document a character's feelings and life.

As well as providing writing practice that builds fluency, your students' entries in their character journals can form the raw material for other types of writing. Your students can reread their entries and use what they have said to create new versions or to write sequels to stories. They can write essays, reports, or poetry from the material they have collected in their character journals.

Tips For Success

1. You may want to model a character journal with your entire class before you ask individual students to keep one. Choose a chapter book with a main character who is the same age or approximately the same age as your students. Reading aloud a realistic fiction story that is set in the present day and is about someone who is your students' age is a good way to begin since they will more easily be able to relate to the character's life.

2. To help your students take on another person's point of view as they begin their character journals, share these suggestions:

   • Put yourself in the character's shoes. Create a mental picture of the setting for the story. Visualize yourself dressed as the character dresses. Visualize what you, the character, are currently doing, thinking, and feeling.

- Date each entry using the real or approximate month, day, and year the character would if he or she were keeping the journal.

- Write the chapter or page numbers that correspond to your entries.

- As you write, consider the sights, sounds, and smells in the world around you. Include your responses to these things in your entries.

- Choose at least one thing in each chapter to relate in your entry.

- Use a pen with different colored ink to highlight your own personal thoughts after your character entries.

3. Read a chapter or two a day to your class and then together write a journal entry as the character might. Either use chart paper that students can reread and refer to, or use the overhead projector so that everyone can watch as you transcribe their words. If you use the overhead, your students can help you with spelling and punctuation. Call your students' attention to the form of an entry as well as the message. Transcribing what your students dictate allows you to model for them the process of taking another perspective and creating entries that are descriptive and document the important happenings in a person's life.

4. When your class has kept a journal together, they are ready to keep their own individual character journals. You can share a book orally, as Kim and Nancy did in the classroom examples given previously, list the characters, and let your students choose the one they want to become. Or, you can provide a number of different titles or a number of the same books, all related to your current science or social studies unit, and let your students choose their book and character.

5. Hancock (1993) suggests looking for the following characteristics when selecting books for character journals:

- strong main characters who exhibit growth as the story progresses;

- age level of the main character is similar to the age of the reader;

- series of emotional events and responses occurring throughout the plot;

- text written in the third person.

If you decide to begin with a story that is biography or historical fiction, choose one that will reinforce and extend a content area unit in which your students are involved. For example, if you are studying colonial America, *The Courage of Sarah Noble* by Alice Dalgleish (Scribner, 1954), is an inspiring story of an 8 year-old girl who goes with her father into the wilderness to cook for him as he builds a cabin for their family. This story develops students' understandings of a young girl's fear and courage as they learn about the perils of her life on the frontier.

You might also consider choosing a book that builds appreciation for another culture, perhaps a biography of a person who comes from the same country as one of your students.

6. Finally, remember to plan for sharing. This honors the endeavor, provides oral reading practice, and lets students share

what they have written. Either pair or form small groups and give students time to read their entries to each other. This is especially effective if students are reading different books or keeping journals from the perspective of different characters in the same book. For example, two students sharing their character journals with each other, one journal based on *Sacagawea* and one based on *The Courage of Sarah Noble*, will learn much from each other about the conflicts and support between early frontier people and various Indian tribes.

7. The following list contains examples of biography and historical fiction (for grades 1–4 and grades 5–7) that are good read-alouds.

For Younger Readers

Mr. Mysterious & Company by Sid Fleischman (1962). Boston: Little Brown. In the early west, a delightful family gives magic shows in small towns as they move from Texas to a San Diego ranch.

Little House In the Big Woods by Laura Ingalls Wilder (1932). New York: Harper. The first in a series, this book begins when Laura is 6 and tells of the hardships and difficulties of pioneer life. Others in the series follow the Ingalls girls and the Wilder boys as they grow up.

Thee, Hannah! by Marguerite de Angeli (1949). New York: Doubleday. In this story a young Quaker girl helps a black mother and her child to safety during the Civil War period.

Flight: The Journey of Charles Lindbergh by Robert Burleigh (1991). New York: Philomel. In this example of courage and endurance, Lindbergh makes his 33 hour flight alone across the Atlantic.

Lost Star: The Story of Amelia Earhart by Patricia Lauber (1988). New York: Scholastic. An exciting story of the famous female aviator who disappeared while trying to fly around the world.

Emily by Michael Bedard (1992). New York: Doubleday. This is the story of poet Emily Dickinson's life, filled with music and mystery and set in 19th century Massachusetts.

For Middle and Older Readers

Sojourner Truth: Ain't I a Woman? by Patricia McKissack (1992). New York: Scholastic. Quotes from Sojourner Truth's autobiography dramatically reveal this legendary black woman.

The Witch of Blackbird Pond by Elizabeth G. Speare (1958). Boston: Houghton Mifflin. Kit Tyler does not follow the beliefs or ways of the Puritan aunt and uncle with whom she lives in 18th century Connecticut.

Roll of Thunder, Hear My Cry by Mildred Taylor (1976). New York: Dial. This is the story of Cassie Logan and her family's experience as blacks in rural Mississippi during the 1930's.

Journey To Topaz by Yoshiko Uchida (1971). New York: Scribner. The story of the American treatment of a young Japanese girl, Yuki, and her family who spend time in an internment camp in Utah during World War II.

Sing Down the Moon by Scott O'Dell (1970). Boston: Houghton Mifflin. This book describes the "Long Walk," a 300 mile forced march of the Navajo from their canyon homes to Fort Sumner, by a woman named Bright Morning.

Apple Is My Sign by Mary Riskind (1981). Boston: Houghton Mifflin. Harry, a 10 year-old deaf child from a deaf family goes away to school in the early 1900's and meets many obstacles.

You can obtain other titles of excellent biographies and historical fiction from children's literature texts such as:

Children and Books, 7th ed. by Zena Sutherland annd May Hill Arbuthnot (1986). Glenview, IL: Scott Foresman.

Children's Literature in the Elementary School, 4th ed. by Charlotte Huck, Susan Hepler and Janet Hickman (1987). Chicago: Holt.

References

Hancock, M.R. (1993). Character journals: Initiating involvement and identification through literature. *Journal of Reading, 37*, 1, 42–53.

Rosenblatt, L.M. (1985). The transactional theory of the literary work: Implications for research. In C.R. Cooper (Ed.), *Researching Response to Literature and the teaching of Literature: Points of Departure* (pp. 33–53). Norwood, NJ: Ablex.

Writer's Journal

A writer's journal is a "potpourri of disparate thoughts, questions and musings"   (Harwayne, 1992).

The substance and form of a writer's journal vary with the person who keeps one. But the purpose of every writer's journal or notebook is the same. It is to provide a private place in which prospective writers can observe, record, collect, analyze, create, compare, uncover, capture, and evaluate their world in preparation for moving into larger writing projects.

The writer's journal or notebook is slightly different than the personal journal (see Chapter 3). The writer's journal is a springboard to writing. It usually provides the preparation and raw material for writing a more cohesive, formal, and longer piece than that of the typical entry. The personal journal is a record or account of happenings, observations, and reflections that is not usually meant to result in other writing.

In the following excerpts, two established authors talk about how the writer's journal acts as a catalyst for their writing. Both show how the particular journal or notebook they kept helped them become a better writer.

Phyllis Reynolds Naylor, author of more than 50 books for children and adults including *Shiloh*, the 1992 Newbery Medal Winner, says that most of her books begin years before they are ever written. She keeps notebooks, with the name of a book-to-be in masking tape on the spine, that have pockets into which she puts photos, newspaper clippings, maps, letters and anything that will help with her writing. About the lined pages of the notebooks she says:

Whenever I get another idea about plot or characters, theme or mood, I just jot it down on the pages of the notebooks so that, when the excitement about a particular book boils over and I'm ready to begin, I already have pages and pages filled with things I will use in my story. (Naylor, 1992).

Novelist Jessamyn West, who has written many books for adult readers, says:

People who keep journals live life twice. Having written something down gives you the opportunity to go back to it over and over, to remember and relive the experience. Keeping a journal can also help you get perspective on your experiences. Sometimes writing something down, like talking about it, helps you understand it better. (West, 1957).

You can see that the form of each of these journals is different. Naylor kept a two-part notebook or album. As well as writing her thoughts and ideas in this notebook, Naylor actually collected realia related to the story she was planning and kept them in pockets in the notebook. West describes a strictly journal-type format in which she transcribed her thoughts and did not collect other materials.

Introducing Writers' Journals

Perhaps in order to foster originality and creativity, we are told that "each person must carefully choose the form his or her notebook will take" (Calkins, 1991). If you ask your students to choose their own writer's journal or notebook, they will probably surprise you by bringing to school a variety of styles such as spiral notebooks, marble-covered composition books, bound volumes, steno pads, and handmade journals with cloth or laminated covers. Whatever the form, it is important that each of your students feels comfortable and at home with his journal. As well, it is important that each student view the writer's journal as a new way of thinking about the writing process.

What does "a new way of thinking about the writing process" mean? It means that the journal can be an invitation to create a treasure chest of ideas and observations from which your students can choose something significant to develop and write about in a writing project that has scope and significance (Calkins, 1991). In their journals, your students will create word pictures they can use in future writing.

One way to help your students begin their writer's journals is to read a book or books about family or the past, such as *The Relatives Came* (Bradbury, 1985) or *When I Was Young In the Mountains* (Dutton, 1982), both by Cynthia Rylant. These stories are appropriate for all ages—they trigger memories and feelings that everyone has and that you can urge students to capture in their journals. Even first graders have little trouble remembering things that happened to them when they were "young." These isolated events, once recorded, may become topics for longer stories or provide brief "flashbacks" experienced by characters in stories. Every children's book can potentially provide images and experiences to be recorded or responded to in writer's journals.

There are also many books about the lives of published authors that you might want to share with your students. In *How I Came To Be a Writer* (Aladdin, 1981) Phyllis Reynolds Naylor humorously describes her experiences with the writing process from the spark of an idea to a book's actual publication. It is illustrated with photos and includes samples of her writing from as early as kindergarten to her more recent work. In *My Widening World* Naylor describes in diary form her career in New York City in the 1920's, her marriage to a young engineer, and the beginning of a new life in England in 1929.

Another way to help students realize that they have unique ways of seeing the world and describing their perceptions is to have them take a visual "snapshot" and record it in their journals. You can ask your students to choose an experience, occasion or scene and capture as many of the visual details as they can. For example, your students might describe a party, a favorite food, an accident, a nature scene, or a place they have visited recently. Remind them to describe the activities, objects, shapes, light, colors, and shades appearing in their snapshot.

Encourage students to sharpen their senses by including more than visual aspects in their snapshots. After they have described what they see in the scene, tell them to consider the sounds they might hear if they were there, the smells and aromas they might be aware of, what things might taste like if there are foods in their snapshot, and the textures or feel of objects or things in the snapshot. The purpose of this activity is to create visual and sensory images with words.

Using a Writer's Journal

One way to help your students keep and use writer's journals effectively is to keep one yourself and share it with them. In it you can model the many different kinds of entries they can make. Several ideas follow for different kinds of entries:

- memories
- dreams, daydreams, and nightmares
- opinions
- images
- impressions
- experiences
- conversations
- lists
- expressions
- quotes
- letters

You can show students how to identify a common theme among a number of entries that might then be expanded into larger pieces of writing. You can show them how you search and reread your own entries for an especially effective ways of expressing feelings or describing incidents. Or, you can show them how you revise and rework an existing entry to make it more powerful or clear.

When your students record images and impressions such as these, the entries can then be revisited and reworked to make them more vivid and powerful. In this way you can help your students experiment and play with language as they refine and recast the word pictures they create. They can then include these bits of description in their future writing.

Another way to help your students use their writer's journals is to make time for them to reread their entries and share favorite or special entries with each other. This can occur in pairs, small groups, or with the whole class. Rereading and sharing validates each student's work. It also invites collaborative writing projects among your students as they discover similarities in their entries and writing styles.

You can also look for areas in which your students need direct instruction and plan mini-lessons based on what you see in their journals. Pam, a fifth grade teacher, noticed that several of her students were keeping word lists in their writer's journals. She decided that a mini-lesson on vocabulary knowledge and usage could extend these students' thinking and language knowledge. She used a list she had been keeping in her journal of different ways to say "jail" eg. "hoosegow," "prison," "penal institution," "reformatory," "penitentiary," "lockup," "pen" and "slammer." When she shared her list with the group, a Mexican student added "calaboose" to the list, explaining that it was a derivation of the Spanish word "calabozo" which means dungeon. With a dictionary and through discussion, the group discovered the shades of difference in meaning between "penitentiary" and "reformatory," and the informal terms "slammer" and "hoosegow." Using a dictionary of word and phrase origins (Morris, 1962), Pam showed her students that "hoosegow" was a corruption of "jusgado," a Spanish word for jailhouse.

Pam suggested her students reread the word lists in their journals and think about how they might expand them in similar ways. She asked her students to share their findings with the group. Following this mini-lesson, one of Pam's students, Jason, made a list in his journal of different ways to talk about death. He used a dictionary, thesaurus, and popular slang, including "die," "depart," "expire," "perish," "decline," "ebb," "subside," "wane," "kick the bucket," "pass away," "pass on," "buy the ranch" and "enter the Pearly Gates."

From this list, Jason noticed that certain words suggested imminent death such as "subside" and "wane," while other words were gentle ways of communicating finality, such as "pass away" or "pass on," and still other sayings were confusing, such as "buy the ranch" and "kick the bucket." So, he used a dictionary of word and phrase origins to discover their meanings. For example, Jason found that "buy the ranch" originated during the Civil War when soldiers talked about what they would do when the war was over. It was often a soldier's dream to go home, buy a ranch, and settle down with his sweetheart, thus when a soldier was killed his friends said he had "bought the ranch."

The list Jason created, the observations he made about the words, and the research he did formed the basis for an essay he wrote that was published in his class newspaper. For Jason, the writer's notebook functioned as a way to record, analyze, research, and compare ideas and finally create something new. For Pam, the notebook and this mini-lesson functioned as a way to help her students launch a study of language and broaden their vocabulary knowledge.

Of course, this is only one example of the kinds of mini-lessons you might derive from your students' writer's journals. Lessons on descriptions, similes, metaphors, dialogue, characterization, and so on are other possibilities. In conferences with individual students, you can also read through individual student's journal entries with them to help them identify themes that they might then write about drawing on material they have already written in their journal. Or, you might show students how entries they may have overlooked could bring life and new meaning to stories they are currently working on.

Tips For Success

Here are some suggestions to share with your students to help them have success with their writer's journals:

1. Don't be afraid to be yourself. You can be sentimental, melodramatic, maudlin, hilarious or serious. In fact it's probably a good idea to record the thoughts you have when you feel different moods. Over the course of a year you may fill many journals with your thoughts. Keep these journals for reference and so that you have a record of your writing.

2. Write all the time and any time. Keep your journal on your desk and carry it with you so you can jot down ideas or feelings on-the-spot as you experience them. This way you record real and vivid bits of your life.

3. Don't worry about spelling and grammar. Your journal is a place to experiment and rehearse. You can rework and revise later or when you have used the ideas in a larger project and are ready to polish it.

4. Reread your journal often for ideas and images to expand and use in the writing project in which you are currently involved. Look for recurring themes in your entries that may give you ideas for a stories.

5. Look back at your first journal entries occasionally and compare them to what and how you are writing now. This will give you an idea of how you are changing as a writer and how your powers of observation and reflection are growing.

6. For in-depth discussions of the writer's journal, you and your students can read Chapter 4, "The Notebook: A Tool for Writing and Living," in *Living Between the Lines* (Calkins & Harwayne, 1991) and Chapter 3, "The Writer's Journal" in *The Young Writer's Handbook* (Tchudi & Tchudi, 1984).

References

Calkins, L. M., & Harwayne, S. (1991). *Living Between the Lines*. Portsmouth, NH: Heinemann.

Harwayne, S. (1992). *Lasting Impressions*. Portsmouth, NH: Heinemann.

Morris, W. (1962) (Ed.) *Morris Dictionary of Word and Phrase Origins*. New Your: HarperCollins.

Naylor, P.R. (1992). The writing of *Shiloh*. *The Reading Teacher*, 46, 1, 10–12.

CHAPTER 14

Electronic Journal

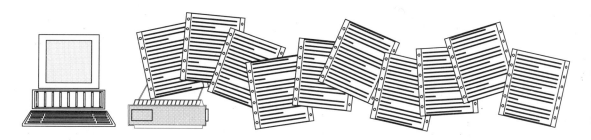

For many students, computers are exciting technological tools that stimulate interest in writing and result in improved writing performance.

Computers are used in classrooms across the country for language learning, computation and problem solving in math, explorations in social studies and science and instruction in reading, as well. It is not uncommon to see children as young as kindergarten age scheduled regularly for time in their school's computer lab. Developing keyboarding skills and computer literacy are goals of most elementary schools today.

Telecommunications is one way for you to create enthusiasm for literacy learning, provide your students with practice in reading and writing, and develop their computer skills. Telecommunication is the transfer of information over distances using computers and telephone lines. When two people correspond via computer, they write back and forth to each other, each using a computer, a software communication program and a modem, which is a piece of hardware that connects a computer to a telephone line. This kind of electronic dialoguing can have a powerful impact on the attitudes and writing performance of your students because it provides a distant but real and interactive audience for the writer.

Electronic Journals For Students

Judy Rickard, a grade 7–9 resource room teacher, reports that her students in Halifax, Nova Scotia, derived many benefits from their computer correspondence with students in Salem, Oregon (Figure 14.1)

From: LAKE KIDS
To: HALIFAX KIDS
Subj: att:modem pals help

Hi kids!

My teacher will be traveling to Nova Scotia, PEI, New Brunswick, etc. this summer. What places would you recommend that she visit in Halifax? Can you tell us some of the sights that she should see, also if you can tell us any of the history of your city. That would be nice. Thank you for your help.

Margie

From: HALIFAX KIDS
To: LAKE KIDS
Subj: reply

Hi Margie!

My name is Terri and my friend is Amanda. We heard that your teacher will be coming to Nova Scotia and we thought she would like to hear what was going on in Halifax in the summer (it would be best to come in August). There is a group of people who come to Halifax and put on different shows such as juggling, flame throwing, and singing.

A good place to start seeing Halifax is to go to a star shaped fort named Citadel Hill down town near the waterfront. Halifax is a peninsula shaped like a shoe. On the toe of the shoe is the lovely Point Pleasant Park.

The population of the Halifax Metropolitan area is 300,000. And we are known as Haligonians. Prince Edward decided that the Citadel Hill needed a large clock to tell everyone in Halifax the time. The clock has 4 faces pointing North, South, East, West.

It would also be fun to go on a ferry across to Dartmouth, a twin city that is attached by two bridges.

We hope she enjoys her trip to Nova Scotia.

Your friends,
Terri and Amanda

14.1 Electronic correspondence between students in Michigan and Nova Scotia.

(Newman, 1989). Judy's students began to revise and edit their own messages for clarity and readability. Their research skills grew as they sought information about their community's history to share with their buddies. Their self-esteem and competence as writers grew, as well. Her students' responses reflect these benefits:

Talking to far-away kids is fun, you learn lots of neat things.

I like finding out about the places they're from.

I have learned a whole lot of stuff about where I live because those kids are interested.

When a school and university shared a telecommunication link, electronic dialogues between fifth graders and graduate students had several positive benefits, also (Moore, 1991). For a semester, fifth graders were matched with teachers who were taking a course called "The Reading/Writing Connection." Partners used their electronic journals to interact socially and to discuss specific children's books.

As the program progressed, the fifth graders' motivation and interest in sharing ideas increased, they wrote more, and their confidence and motivation to read and write increased. Their electronic journal experience helped these students relate setting, characters, plot, and events of the story to their personal lives and resulted in improved understanding of the stories. Their teachers saw the relationship between reading and writing more clearly and became more comfortable with computers. For both the students and teachers, the purpose of this literacy activity and the real audience electronic journals provided were important.

How do you find "electronic" journal partners for your students? Start your search close to home. There may be students within your own school system with whom your students can correspond, as long as each classroom or school is networked. Schools in neighboring districts are also a possibility, offering the opportunity of longer distance correspondence.

Another way to find an audience is by looking into online services. Scholastic Network (800–246–2986), a highly interactive online service, is designed especially for teachers and students. With access to a computer, a modem, and a telephone line (at home or at school), you and your students can connect with an international learning community. For example, in the network's reading and language arts section, your students can share and exchange writings, including journals, with children in classrooms across the country. You can use the Professional Conferences area to share ideas for using journals with other teachers. In addition, the teaching with Technology area lets you exchange ideas for keeping electronic portfolios, including those with a journal component. You can even set up your own journal exchanges with colleagues across the country. Other online services, such as FrEd Mail Network (619–475–4852) offer similar opportunities for electronic journal experiences.

With today's telecommunication capabilities, students can collaborate and communicate with their peers in the next state or on the opposite side of the globe. Future possibilities for telecommunication systems

JOURNAL ENTRY #4 10-26

The students loved the idea of Writing Roulette and had fun playing it. Julie and I made it clear that they were to be kept clean and that they were to create a STORY, but regardless, we got some questionable material. Are homosexual encounters really appropriate material to write about in school? Not to mention the fact that they were quite homophobic in nature. On top of that, the violence in them was disturbing to me. What does a teacher do when subjects such as these come up? Much of the violence was also directed at women. Do we ignore it and chalk it up to their age and the sign of the times? When I told a friend about the incident she replied, "Look what they are exposed to on T.V. Why are you so surprised?" Hmmmmm..........

As far as the lesson was concerned, there was a glimmer of light within all of this. One group mimicked the style of The Frog Prince Continued. To me this was incredible. I've read about children connecting their reading and their writing, but I got to see/read first hand this time. Secondly, the students' excitement when we explained Writing Roulette can't be ignored just because the writing we got was, well, questionable. The way the game works, all it takes is one rotten egg to spoil it all. They were genuinely excited about writing and I believe it was because they could write what they wanted to. Somehow modifying the game/lesson so they can still writie what they want, but produce a bit more quality would be good, but I'm not quite sure how....

--Deborah

14.2–14.4 Deborah keeps a journal in which she documents and reflects on her teaching.

are even more exciting. Electronic dialogue journals are just the tip of the iceberg!

Electronic Journals For Teachers

If you have a computer and word processing software in your classroom, don't overlook the potential they have for making your instruction more effective. Deborah, a graduate student with a degree in English, used an electronic journal to document and reflect on the teaching she and Julie, a business education teacher, did together as part of a graduate course they were taking. They team taught a unit integrating computer applications and creative writing.

JOURNAL ENTRY #10 11-10

They are finishing up their rough drafts and some have mentioned that they know how they are going to start laying out their text and what fonts they are going to use. They really seem to be integrating the language arts and the computer applications. Thank goodness!

I mentioned to a few of them while conferencing with the groups that if any of them are interested in trying to publish their stories, I'd be more than happy to help them find a publisher to send their stories to. Some seemed excited by the idea, but I'm not sure there will be any takers.

Tomorrow is finishing up the rough drafts and lines, boxes and borders. The rest of our time will be spent working to put all the pieces together---fixing up the drafts and making changes, laying out the text, trying out different fonts, text in and out of borders etc. I pray we can get this done by the end of next week---the end of the marking period approaches!

--Deborah

14.3
14.4

JOURNAL ENTRY #11 11-12

It finally hit me today---we're four weeks into this unit and 75% of our time revolved around reading and writing about/of children's stories as opposed to reading or writing about computer related material. When we planned the unit, Julie and I did this intentionally since there was no book for her computer applications class. I don't know if this was the best way to arrange this unit. There were limitations that we've had to work with ie. no book, lack of typing skills, and the biggest one: In an ideal situation, this would be an integrated unit in an English class and a computer applications class, giving us the time to expand the unit.

Is the fact that we've spent a good chunk of our time on non-computer type thing a horrible occurrence? I'm not convinced either way. I think there were a lot of benefits to it as well as a lot of draw backs.

As far as the benefits are concerned, the students learned what it was like to compose on a computer, to edit on hard and soft copy, the value of saving a project on a disc as opposed to paper and word processing all because of their time spent composing the children's story. Granted, this learning didn't come from direct instruction in computers, but they learned it through experience.

As far as draw backs are concerned, at times it felt like an English class and not a computers class. I started to wonder if the students were getting all they needed as far as the computer curriculum was concerned. Was working on the writing so much holding Julie back from going further in depth on desk top publishing? I can't help but think about all the extra time that could have been used if this was taught as an integrated unit between an English class and a computer class with two periods a day available instead of one.

Should I ever have the opportunity, I would want to teach this type of integrated unit in a truly integrated fashion. At least I have a base to work from should the time ever come.

--Deborah

The unit involved putting students in cooperative groups so they could study examples of quality picture books for children. Then each group used what they had learned to plan their own stories. They drafted, revised, edited, and published their stories using word processing and desktop publishing. Another class created illustrations. Deborah's and Julie's students proudly shared their stories with children in the elementary school before the books became part of the school's library collection.

Deborah took a few minutes at the end of each day's lesson to document what had occurred that day and to enter her thoughts, impressions, and questions in her electronic journal (Figures 14.2–14.4).

Because of this reflection, Deborah was more intentional about what she was doing and better able to articulate what she learned.

Some teachers keep electronic journals like Deborah's, but use them to record their impressions of various students and progress or difficulties they are having. Electronic journals can help with your "kid-watching," and give you an easily accessible and readable record to use in planning instruction or to share with individual students and parents.

Tips For Success

1. To learn more about electronic journals read:

- "Telecommunications in the Reading Classroom" by Robert Rickelman and William Henk in *The Reading Teacher* (1991), *43*, 6, 418–19;

- The "Technology Links to Literacy" department featured each month in *The Reading Teacher* to keep abreast of telecommunications in the classroom;
- *EDUCOM Review*, a journal dedicated to technology and electronic news that is directly related to curriculum and instruction.

2. Use electronic jourals to motivate students for whom writing is difficult. Keyboarding may be easier than handwriting for some. Removing some of the frustration of writing and appealing to students' natural interest in technology, may generate increased enthusiasm for journal writing.

References

Moore, M.A. (1991). Electronic dialoguing: An avenue to literacy. *The Reading Teacher*, *45*, 4, 280–286.

Newman, J.M. (1989). Online: From far away. *Language Arts*, *66*, 7, 791–797.

CHAPTER 15

Daily Group Journal

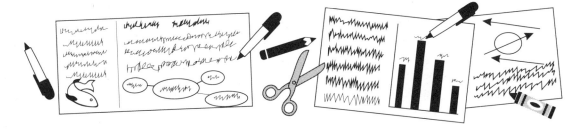

In the past, the Language Experience Approach (LEA) has been a popular and universally used method for developing language knowledge and teaching young children to read.

The basic components of an LEA lesson are: a shared experience, group discussion, student dictation, teacher transcription, teacher reading, group reading and individual re-reading. LEA is based on the idea that when children talk about an experience or activity, what they say can be written down and read back to them. The goal of LEA, which involves dictation by the child to the teacher who is the scribe, is to build children's oral language competence and help them see the link between spoken and written language.

In recent years, the advent of an emergent literacy perspective and research on the writing process has raised several questions about LEA (Strickland & Morrow, 1990). How can children develop a sense of ownership of their writing if the teacher always

writes for them? How effective is it to have the teacher continually model proper letter formation, spelling, and sentence construction? What do children learn about language and literacy from experimenting with written language and transcribing themselves? Will children take risks and attempt invented spelling when they have only been exposed to the standard spelling of teacher transcription?

Rather than replacing the old methodology with the new, it is important to recognize the contributions of each to children's literacy development. It only makes sense to combine the strengths of both approaches. LEA provides opportunities for lots of talk about shared experiences and models of standard form and spelling, both critical to emerging readers and writers. Independent writing by children provides opportunities for firsthand experimentation with print, risk-taking, and status as individual work is recognized and shared.

One way to combine group dictation and teacher transcription with independent writing is through a daily group journal (Strickland & Morrow, 1990). Daily group journals engage young children in nonthreatening, purposeful literacy activities as they move toward independence in reading and writing. With a daily group journal, both children's dictated and transcribed language and their individual attempts at writing are valued and celebrated. These oral and written language compostions then form the basis for the print children will learn to read. In this way, you encourage language development in natural and meaningful ways as children create and use whole text.

Following are strategies and suggestions to help you make and use this type of journal with your students:

1. **Create experiences.** Both planned and unplanned activities and engagements that you plan for your children are valuable sources for thinking and talking. A trip to the police station, a seashell, or some other object a student has brought to school can form the experience and basis for discussion.

2. **Foster discussion and dictation.** During and after the experience it is important to allow and encourage your children to make observations, share opinions, and in general, talk about their feelings and reactions. Take every opportunity to reinforce and extend the vocabulary they use.

3. **Use transcription to model.** You can model the writing process as you transcribe children's oral language into their group journal:
   - Pause to allow children to predict the next word or letter.
   - Think aloud about the message and language that is being used.
   - Revise and edit while the children watch.

4. **Practice reading and rereading.** Read the class story then allow children to "echo" read with you, reading orally together after you have read to them. Encourage children to look for letters and words they know, words that repeat, or other interesting print.

5. **Encourage independent drawing and writing.** You can have your children draw or write their own journal entries that grow from topics in daily journals. This can occur as a whole group activity or at a center where your children choose what they will do. You can collate these pages into a book, combine them in a notebook, or keep them together in a folder.

6. **Celebrate by sharing.** If you write group entries on chart paper, you can clip them to a wire hanger and hang them on a metal rack for later rereading. You can laminate the pages or make a cover from paper bags that your children will enjoy decorating. Children can share their individual entries with a peer and/or you. To encourage beginning writers, be sure to give positive reinforcement for scribbling, drawing, and invented spelling.

Variations

Across the Grades

Don't overlook the possibility of using the daily group journal with older students as well as younger children. A variation for fifth and sixth grade students is a class poetry journal in which students respond to poetry, write their own, revise, and publish it (McClure, 1990). Older students also enjoy creating original lyrics for popular or well-known songs. It is a natural springboard for writing original music and lyrics as well.

A variation for all grades is a class journal in which students document the activities of the class around a particular project or unit of study. Entries might alternate between group composed and those composed by individuals. The finished product can go home with students who want to share it with their families. This connection with your students' homes can be an effective way to let parents see their children's work and keep them informed about what is going on in school at the same time.

Especially for ESL Students and Struggling Readers and Writers

Daily group journals hold rich potential for helping students who have limited English proficiency. A class journal provides the same opportunities and benefits for these students as it does for young children. It allows students who are learning English as a second language to participate and develop literacy at their own rates and levels of ability. They can hear and see their own language being used at once and have multiple opportunities to revisit it. As a result, the sight and meaning vocabularies of these students will grow.

You can use poem picture books effectively with ESL students and young beginning readers and writers as a shared experience and basis for group journal entries. A poem picture book is actually a poem that has been reprinted and illustrated in book form. Why are they particularly useful with these children? This type of literature is rhythmic, predictable, and repetitive, all characteristics that make it easily readable.

After reading a poem picture book to your class, students can share responses to the poems and pictures and you can record these in the group journal. Or, as children read a poem line-by-line, you can transcribe the poems themselves into the group journal for later individual reading or group choral reading.

Another type of picture book that has similar advantages for ESL learners and beginning readers and writers is the song picture book. Song picture books are songs that have been illustrated and published in book form. This type of literature, too, is rhythmic, predictable, and repetitive, and thus more easily read by ESL students and beginning readers and writers.

For these students, song picture books have the added allure of music. The musical element of these books invites your students' involvement. First, listen to a recording or teach your children how to sing the song. When they have heard the song and learned to sing it, transcribe the lyrics into their group journal, and use them for repetitive listening, singing, and reading. Once your children know the song lyrics you can help them see patterns of rhyming words and numbers of syllables in words. They can create new lyrics in their group journal for everyone to sing and read together. Original song parodies are favorites.

The following is a sampling of some of the poem and song picture books that are available:

Poem Picture Books

Hawk, I'm Your Brother by Byrd Baylor (1986). New York: Scribner.

Stopping By Woods on a Snowy Evening by Robert Frost (1978). New York: Dutton.

Birches by Robert Frost (1988). New York: Holt, Rinehart & Winston.

The Owl and the Pussycat by Edward Lear (1988). New York: Warne.

Walking To School by Elizabeth Turner (1989). New York: Orchard.

For other titles of poem picture books and further ideas for using them in your classroom, see the article by Joan Glazer and Linda Lamme, "Poem Picture Books and Their Uses in the Classroom," in *The Reading Teacher*, (1990) Volume 42, pp. 102–109.

Song Picture Books

Tortillas Para Mama by M. Greigo (1980). New York: Holt, Rinehart & Winston.

Moonsong Lullaby by J. Highwater (1981). New York: Morrow.

Roll Over! A Counting Song by M. Peek (1981). New York: Houghton Mifflin.

Hush Little Baby by Aliki Brandenberg (1978). Englewood Cliffs, NJ: Prentice Hall.

This Old Man by P. Adams (1975). New York: Grossett & Dunlap.

If You're Happy and You Know It by N. Weiss (1987). New York: Greenwillow.

Other titles of song picture books and ideas for using them in your classroom can be found in an article by Linda Lamme, "Exploring the World of Music Through Picture Books" in *The Reading Teacher*, (1990) Volume 44, pp. 294–301.

Tips For Success

1. Keep enthusiasm for daily group journals high by incorporating a variety of types of entries. In addition to narrative accounts, you might try lists, line-a-child reactions, recipes, directions, notices and signs, lyrics, poems and charts, and observations about a class pet or plant.

2. When recording children's contributions on chart paper, skip lines between entries to facilitate inserting revisions and additions.

3. To build ownership, use markers of different colors for each child's entry. Write students' initials or names after their entries for easier identification.

4. Invite children to add pictures and drawings to the text they create to aid in rereading.

References

McClure, A.A. (1990). *Sunrises and Songs*. Portsmouth, NH: Heinemann.

Strickland, D.S., & Morrow, L.M. (1990). The daily journal: Using languge experience strategies in an emergent literacy curriculum. *The Reading Teacher, 43*, 422–423.

CHAPTER 16

Nurturing Journal Writers

Not every student is enthusiastic about journal writing all the time. In fact, some students "run out of gas" when it comes to daily journal writing.

When you sense that your students are beginning to "run on the fumes"—entries are short or nonexistent, seem mechanical or routine, and your students audibly sigh at the mention of journals—there are things you can do to nurture the journal writers in your classroom.

Ownership is probably the key word, both in getting journals off to a strong start and in keeping journals going. Ownership depends on the personal connection that exists between a person and what is owned. How do you get students to "own" their journals? Allow them to:

- select their own journals or make their own and decorate the covers;
- choose the tools they write with in their journals;

- choose their own topics;
- write without fear of being judged or graded.

Ownership grows as a result of enjoyment. For some students the act of writing will be satisfaction enough. For other students, an appreciative audience—you and others with whom your students share occasional entries—is important, because it gives writers the pleasure and satisfaction of being listened to. Feedback that is positive and appreciative helps give your writers a feeling of worth as well.

Valuing also plays a role in ownership. When your students recognize the value of writing in journals, they are more apt to do it and to become personally involved. You can help students understand the value of journal writing by talking with them about the function of journals. You can also read excerpts from children's literature in which main characters write in journals or authors talk about how journals function for them and why they keep journals.

Another way to help your students discover the benefits of journals is to have them examine and evaluate selected entries from published journals. Read entries or reproduce pages for children to read from books like *Dear Mr. Henshaw* by Beverly Cleary (Morrow, 1984), *Anastasia, Ask Your Analyst* by Lois Lowery (Houton Mifflin, 1984), and *The Diary of Young Girl*, by Anne Frank (Washington Press, 1987). Then, as entries in their own journals, have students describe the benefits of journal writing for Leigh Botts, Anastasia, or Anne Frank. Ask questions that encourage students to consider both personal and academic advantage, for example:

- How did journal writing help _____ grow as a person?

- How did journal writing help _____ solve problems?

- How did journal writing help _____ with school work?

- How did journal writing help _____ in other ways?

Follow up by helping students find the value in their own journals. Students can use the questions that follow as starters for examining and evaluating their journals:

- What have I learned about myself from my journal entries?

- What have I learned about my life? My dreams? My fears?

- What have I learned about myself as a writer? Reader?

- Which is my favorite entry? Why?

- Which is my least favorite entry? Why?

- What does writing in my journal do for me?

- An example of how my journal writing has helped me in another subject is. . .

As well as value and content, another aspect of journals that can be evaluated is handwriting. You might ask students to rate the legibility of their handwriting in three separate entries chosen from the beginning, middle, and end of their journals. They can even discuss this rating of their legibility in a journal entry. Students might also describe, in a journal entry, the aspect of handwriting legibility they are most pleased with and something they want to change or improve, for example, letter shape, size and proportion, spacing, slant, steadiness of line, and style.

Examining their own entries can also build and reinforce students' math and research skills. Using their own journal entries, students can practice counting, recording, and graphing. Part way through the year and at the end of the year, they can count and record the number of entries written per month. Or, they can record different kinds of entries made throughout the journal. For example, some students use their journals as personal journals for a time, then the journals become learning logs for awhile. Students can create graphs or pie charts to represent their findings. You might invite students to talk about what they discover. For example, does the frequency of entries increase or decrease over time? What might this indicate?

You may still have a few questions about nurturing the journal writers in your classroom. If you do, the following questions and answers may help clear up any uncertainties you may have.

Q: Can journals really accomplish all they seem to promise?

A: Journals are only one avenue for helping students reflect on their own learning, gain insights, and build written fluency. Your writing program should include many other audiences and forms of writing.

Q: Is it important for students to have goals for their journal writing?

A: Yes, having students establish their goals for journals or setting some up in collaboration with you is an excellent way to build ownership and ensure success.

Q: What is the biggest problem teachers encounter with journal writing?

A: The biggest problem is a lack of time. To succeed, you need to consistently set aside a certain time every day or every other day, and honor this commitment.

Q: At what age or grade level are journals best introduced and used?

A: Children are ready as soon as they show enough small muscle coordination to make marks on paper and have an interest in scribbling or drawing. Through journals you can foster emergent writing with young children and encourage reading and writing development with ESL students or students with learning disabilities.

Q: How do I get started with journal writing in my classroom?

A: First, be sure to brainstorm rules together with students and post them so students know what you expect. For example:

- Date each entry.
- Take time to think before you write.
- Write for at least 10 minutes.
- Write at least 3 sentences.

Second, brainstorm and list possible topics to write about, or show students how you would write an entry or entries and then write a few entries together as a class.

Q: What part of the day is best for journal writing?

A: The best time for you depends on your daily schedule and the type of journals your students keep. It makes sense to write in learning logs during or right after science, social studies, or math. Home-School journals are probably best written in on Friday or the last day of the week, so the message is fresh and the family can write a response over the weekend. It makes sense to write entries in character journals during or after reading the book in which the character appears.

Q: Is it helpful for me to keep a journal and write with my students?

A: Yes, it shows you value the activity. Keeping a journal is also a way to demonstrate the process. You can share your entries as models.

Q: How do I share literary models with my students? Most of the books in Appendix A seem too difficult for them.

A: Students understand much more than we realize. They can comprehend books and selected entries from books that are written for older students and adults. So, don't avoid occasionally reading books or excerpts from books that are meant for older students, especially if the example or model you share has significance for them.

Q: How do I respond to my students' journals and how often is enough?

A: Respond personally and to the messages they write, not to the mechanics, grammar, or spelling. Respond as frequently as you want to or need to in order to keep in touch with what students are writing.

Q: How many journals do I use at one time?

A: Probably one kind at a time but certainly no more than two or your students will be journaled-out. It's a good idea to check with other teachers your students have to see if anyone else requires journals. Either coordinate journals so only one of you is using them at once or collaborate. For example, integrate learning logs with science, or use character or travel journals in social studies.

Q: How long do students keep a journal?

A: Some teachers have students keep a journal all year long, but vary the kind of journal to keep the writing fresh. For example, use a literature response journal for a few weeks, then try buddy journals or learning logs.

Q: Are certain kinds of journals best for certain age students?

A: Some, such as the draw-and-tell journal, probably work better for younger children, struggling writers, or ESL students. Others, such as the writer's journal, may need the sophistication of older students to be most successful. But, make your own decisions according to your own students and your curricular goals.

Q: What do I do for "tired journals?"

A: Let students draw pictures, maps, or webs; write with different colored pens or pencils; or take a break from journals for awhile.

Q: How do I deal with entries related to abuse, drugs, suicide, sex, or other sensitive topics?

A: First, know what your legal responsibilities are. Talk with your school's principal, psychologist, counselor, and nurse. Talk with the student privately then determine the best course of action. Some teachers involve their school psychologist or counselor in dialogue or buddy journals with special students.

Q: What if students have entries they don't want me to read?

A: Suggest that students fold, staple, or mark VP (for very private) entries they don't want to share.

Q: Can mini-lessons grow out of all kinds of journals?

A: Whatever information you can glean from journals about students' strengths and needs is fair game for mini-lessons. Journals are a good window on your students' thinking and learning processes and can help you shape instruction.

Q: How do I deal with students who are resistant to writing?

A: One of these suggestions is bound to help:

- Involve students in electronic journals. Computers and technology have a magnetic effect on most students.

- Pair them with other students or adults that they have something in common and will want to write to.

- Let them write about self-selected books they have read or topics of interest to them.

- Give them a role in helping you monitor journals, perhaps "being" you and dialoguing with their peers.

Q: How is material in journals best shared?

A: Journals can be shared student to teacher, student to student, student to small group, or sometimes not at all, especially if they are private. It's important to let students volunteer and to offer different ways to share, for example, orally or by passing the journal around in a small group.

Q: Is there an advantage to switching from one journal to another?

A: Yes, changing from one type of journal to another on a regular basis keeps interest high and the momentum for writing going.

Q: How do I deal with evaluation and grades for journals?

A: For best results, avoid grading journals. But you can have students evaluate their own journal writing using the suggestions in this chapter and Chapter Four. You might also require journal writing to receive a grade for reading, language arts, or English, without giving the journal a grade itself. Or, consider giving students a certain number of points for writing in their journals, fewer if they do not write much, and none if they don't write anything.

Q: What subject or content areas lend themselves to journal writing?

A: You can use journals in any subject or content area where you want to encourage thoughtful reflection and engage students in reading, writing, thinking, and learning.

Q: How do journals relate to students' other writing?

A: Writing in journals is only one form of writing and as such is one part of your writing program. Journals can be seen as a bridge to other, more formal, writing.

Q: How can journals contribute to my professional growth?

A: Journals allow you to know your students better and to be a finer teacher. You can use the information in your students' journals to assess students' strengths and needs and to plan more effective instruction. Journals also help you become a better observer and listener. You will know more about your teaching and about how you can help your students become all they are capable of being.

Annotated Bibliography: Journal Writing in Children's Books

For ease of use, this bibliography is arranged alphabetically by author within each of the seven categories discussed in Chapter Two: Present Day Journals, Fantasy Journals, Journals From the Past, Travel Journals, Biography Based on Journals, Journals in Science.

To help guide your selections, each annotation is followed by P (picture book), M (middle reader), or O (older reader). Remember, students of all ages enjoy picture books and you can read difficult books to younger children with excellent results!

Present Day Journals

Adler, D.A. (1985). *Eaton Stanley and the Mind Control Experiment.* **New York: Dutton.**

Two sixth graders, Eaton and Brian, keep a log book and try to control their teacher's mind in this funny adventure. (M)

Byars, B. (1990). *The Burning Questions of Bingo Brown.* **New York: Penguin.**

In this humorous story, sixth grader Harrison (Bingo) Brown, keeps a school journal that he fills with questions about girls, his teacher, wearing t-shirts with print, mousse, mixed-sex conversations, and so on. (M)

Cleary, B. (1984). *Dear Mr. Henshaw.* **New York: Morrow.**

Leigh Botts writes letters to his favorite author and begins his own diary. Through his letters children learn about how Leigh copes with his parents' divorce and his difficulties at school. (M)

Cleary, B. (1991). *Strider.* **New York: Morrow.**

Fourteen-year old Leigh Botts writes a series of diary entries in which he tells about his parents' divorce, how he acquired joint custody of an abandoned dog, and how he joined the track team at school. (M)

Cleary, B. (1984). *The Ramona Quimby Diary*. **New York: Morrow.**

A story and instructions for using the book begin this diary filled with dated spaces designed for writing something special each month. Children can write and draw their own entries. (M)

Colman, H. (1975). *Diary of a Frantic Kid Sister*. **New York: Archway.**

For one year, eleven-year-old Sarah records her mixed feelings about Didi, her 15 year-old sister. Sarah documents how it feels to be a little sister and finally comes to terms with her lack of self confidence. (M)

Cummings, P. (1992). *Petey Moroni's Camp Runamok Diary*. **New York: Bradbury.**

Petey, a young black boy, carries his diary everywhere. Each day tells another adventure with the raccoon at Camp Runamok. (P)

Fitzhugh, L. (1964). *Harriet the Spy*. **New York: Dell.**

Eleven-year-old Harriet spies on people and has fifteen notebooks of funny and caustic observations. She becomes class editor for the school newspaper. (M)

Glasser, D. (1976). *The Diary of Trilby Frost*. **New York: Holiday House.**

A teenage girl, Trilby, keeps a diary about growing up in rural Tennessee at the turn of the century. In it, she comes to realize that life continues even though her father, brother, and best friend die. (O)

Hayes, S. (1981). *Me and My Mona Lisa Smile*. **New York: Lodestar.**

Rowena's poems and journal entries tell the story of a shy girl whose English teacher helps her gain confidence in herself through her writing abilities. (O)

Hooker, R. (1970). *Gertrude Kloppenburg (Private)*. **Nashville: Abingdon.**

A young girl keeps a diary where she explores feelings, dreams, and problems as she searches for a friend at school and at home. Her mother, a bookkeeper in a department store, her neighbors, and friends all appear in her humorous entries. (M)

Hunter, L. (1992). *The Diary of Latoya Hunter*. **New York: Crown.**

This is the true diary of a 12 year-old black girl's first year of junior high school in the Bronx. Friendships, boys, television, and conflcits with her mother are just some of the topics Latoya explores. (M)

Lowry, L. (1986). *Anastasia Has the Answers*. **Boston: Houghton Mifflin.**

Anastasia, an aspiring journalist, keeps a notebook in which she practices writing about her concerns, friends, love, and life. Her journal entries serve as introductions to each of the humorous chapters. (M)

Lowry, L. (1984). *Anastasia, Ask Your Analyst*. **Boston: Houghton Mifflin.**

Anastasia keeps a science project notebook of humorous observations about her gerbils and her personal problems. (M)

Perl, L. (1987). *The Secret Diary of Katie Dinkerhof.* **New York: Scholastic.**

Fourteen year-old Katie lies to her diary, writing what she wishes would happen rather than what does, and learns how to make wishful thinking a reality. (O)

Pfeffer, S.B. (1988). *The Year Without Michael.* **New York: Bantam.**

This journal tells about the disappearance of thirteen year-old Michael and how his family spends months searching and hoping for his return. The family looks to Michael's teenage sister Jody, who keeps the journal, for strength and support. (O)

Robertson, K. (1989). *Henry Reed, Inc.* **New York: Penguin.**

Henry's parents send him to his aunt and uncle's house in New Jersey for the summer. Henry and his neighbor, Midge Glass, form a company called "Reed and Glass, Inc., Pure and Applied Research." Journal entries in this book document their adventures. (M)

Smith, R.K. (1987). *Mostly Michael.* **New York: Delacourte.**

In his diary, Michael records the ups and downs of his eleventh year as he copes with braces, unwelcome relatives, a baby sister, the school play, and a spelling bee. (M)

Tolan, S.S. (1981). *The Last of Eden.* **New York: Scribner.**

Michelle, who loves writing, takes her journal everywhere, even to the beach on Saturday afternoons. (M)

Waber, B. (1970). *Nobody Is Perfick.* **Boston: Houghton Mifflin.**

A boy keeps a notebook with lists of the "Ten-Best." (P)

Zindel, P. (1987). *Amazing and Death Defying Diary of Eugene Dingman.* **New York: Harper Collins.**

Eugene is fifteen. He lives with his mother and older sister and misses his father who left them long ago. In this humorous story, Eugene's diary is his confidant and therapist. He begins each journal entry with trivia and refers to familiar music and tv stars. (O)

Fantasy Journals

Oakley, G. (1987). *The Diary of a Church Mouse.* **New York: Atheneum.**

Humphrey keeps a diary for a year about his life in the Wortlethorpe Church vestry. The humorous escapades of Sampson, the cat, Arthur, and the other church mice are described in detailed text and illustrations. (P)

Van Allsburg, C. (1991). *The Wretched Stone.* **Boston: Houghton Mifflin.**

Excerpts from the log of a ship's captain tell the story of a strange glowing stone that is picked up on a sea voyage and has a terrible transforming effect on the ship's crew. (M)

Jones, R.D. (1993). *The Beginning of Unbelief.* **New York: Atheneum.**

Fifteen-year old Hal keeps a journal and within its pages he creates a science fiction story called "The Beginning of

Unbelief" about his imaginary companion Zach and a spaceship in danger. (O)

Journals from the Past

Blos, J. (1979). *A Gathering of Days.* **New York: Scribner.**

Written in the form of a journal with day-to day entries, this book relates Catherine Hall's life in New England in the 1800's. The diary format communicates her thoughts and feelings and might encourage children to keep their own journals. (O)

Ginsburg, M. (1968). *The Diary of Nina Kosterina.* **New York: Crown.**

This moving document, not intended for publicatin, is the story of an adolescent growing up in soviet Russia during the early days of World War II. Nina began her diary in 1936, when she was 15 years old. It ends with her death at 21. (O)

Hamm, D.J. (1990). *Bunkhouse Journal.* **New York: Scribner.**

In his journal, a 16 year-old boy tells about his first love, his alcoholic father, and life with his cousins on a Wyoming ranch during the winter of 1911. (O)

Hesse, K. (1992). *Letters From Rifka.* **New York: Holt.**

In this journal, a young girl writes to her cousin, describing her family's flight from Russia in 1919 and her experiences when she is left behind in Belgium for awhile when the others emigrate to America. (O)

Johnston, N. (1973). *The Keeping Days.* **New York: Atheneum.**

Over a period of seven-months in 1900, a fourteen year-old girl tells about her family and their collective experiences. (O)

McPhail, D. (1992). *Farm Boy's Year.* **New York: Atheneum.**

In this picture book and journal, a young boy documents his life in the 1800's on a farm in New England. (P)

Orgel, D. (1976). *A Certain Magic.* **New York: Dial.**

Eleven-year old Jenny discovers her aunt's diary and begins a search into her aunt's pre-World War II past. Excerpts from the diary are part of this suspenseful story. (M)

Thaxter, C. (1992). *Celia's Island Journal.* **Boston: Little Brown.**

Lovely illustrations and journal entries by young Celia relate her experiences growing up in the mid 19th century on an island off the coast of New England where her father keeps a lighthouse. (P)

Wilder, L.I. (1986). *The First Four Years.* **New York: HarperCollins.**

This journal tells the story of Laura and Alonzo Wilder's first four years of marriage in which they have a child and are unsuccessful at farming on the South Dakota prairie in the 1800's. (M)

Wilder, L.I. (1962). *On the Way Home.* **New York: HarperCollins.**

This diary of a trip from South Dakota to Mansfield, Missouri, in 1894 tells the trials and triumphs of raising a family on the prairie frontier. (M)

Yezzo, D. (1964). *A GI's Vietnam Diary: 1968-1969.* **New York: Franklin Watts.**

This diary is a moving account of a young soldier's experiences in Vietnam. It reveals a young man's war experiences and his inner conflicts as he reexamines his values. (O)

Travel Journals

Anderson, J. (1987). *Joshua's Westward Journal.* **New York: Morrow.**

Joshua Carpenter keeps a journal as he and his family travel across the prairie through long stretches of empty wilderness in the mid 1800's. They travel in a narrow wooden wagon pulled by horses and packed with food, water, and all their belongings. (P)

Conrad, P. (1991). *Pedro's Journal.* **Honesdale, PA: Caroline House.**

This is the story of Christopher Columbus told from the perspective of young Pedro, a cabin boy aboard the Santa Maria. Sketches and journal entries chronicle Columbus' first voyage.

Harvey, B. (1992). *Cassie's Journey: Going West In the 1860's.* **New York : Holiday House.**

Based on actual women's diaries kept on their westward travels, a young girl relates the hardships and dangers of traveling in a covered wagon from Missouri to California. (P)

Lasky K. (1986). *Beyond the Divide.* **New York: Morrow.**

Fourteen-year old Meribah is from a large Amish family. After her father is shunned by the community she decides to travel west with him in search of a new life. The book is written in journal form and tells about the westward expansion of America during the 1800's. (O)

Lowe, S. (1992). *The Log of Christopher Columbus.* **New York: Philomel.**

The text is an adaptation of excerpts from Columbus' diary, kept on his first voyage to the new world during spring and summer 1492. Entries reveal disappointments, excitement, and fears.

Turner, A. (1987). *Nettie's Trip South.* **New York: Macmillan.**

Based on the real diary of the author's great grandmother, this is an account of one girl's reaction to slavery on her trip from Albany to Richmond. Nettie writes to her friend about the things she saw and heard in the pre-Civil War south. (P)

Biography Based on Journals

Duncan, L. (1949). *Chapters: My Growth As a Writer.* **Boston: Little Brown.**

Excerpts from Lois Duncan's diary and stories she wrote, interspersed with personal anecdotes, help relate the autobiography of this writer's life. (O)

Frank, A. (1987). *The Diary of a Young Girl.* **Philadelphia: Washington Square Press.**

Thirteen-year-old Anne keeps a diary of events she and her family endure while hiding from the Nazis during World War II in Germany. (M)

Frank, A. (1987). *The Diary of a Young Girl.* **Cornerstone.**
> This is a large type reproduction of the 1947 edition. (M)

Keyes, D. (1970). *Flowers for Algernon.* **New York: Bantam.**
> Thirty-three-year-old Charlie is a retarded bakery laborer who keeps a journal about his experiences. Through an experimental operation and with the help of his teacher, doctors, and scientists, he gains artificial intelligence. (O)

Meigs, C. (1933). *Invincible Louisa.* **Boston: Little, Brown.**
> This biography of Louisa May Alcott's life emphasizes her devotion to family and her great love of reading and writing. She writes poetry, stories, and a journal before earning an income as a writer. (M)

Miller, R. (1986). *Robyn's Book: A True Diary.* **New York: Scholastic.**
> Twenty-one year old Robyn, a cystic fibrosis patient, has created a collection of personal writings. In this personal journal she includes poems, personal histories, and short stories about her friends and information about her disease. (O)

Yates, E. (1983). *My Widening World: The Continuing Diary of Elizabeth Yates.* **Philadelphia: Westminister Press.**
> This is the journal of a young writer who begins her career in New York City in the 1920's. It details her marriage to a young engineer and the beginning of a new life in England in 1929. (O)

Yates, E. (1981). *My Diary-My World.* **Philadelphia: Westminster.**
> This is the diary of a writer from the time she was twelve until she was almost twenty. It tells the story of a young girl's determination to become a writer despite her family's objections. Elizabeth Yates went on to write *Amos Fortune, Free Man* and twenty-five other books. (O)

Journals in Science

Brenner, B. (1970). *A Snake Lover's Diary.* **New York: Harper Collins.**
> During a spring and summer, a young boy keeps a diary, complete with photos, of the physical characteristics and habitat of the reptiles he catches. (M)

Heinrich, B. (1990). *An Owl In the House: A Naturalist's Diary.* **Boston: Little Brown.**
> This field journal, with drawings and photos, tracks the development of a great horned owlet rescued in the wild as it becomes an independent hunter able to survive in its own habitat. (O)

Directions For Making Journals

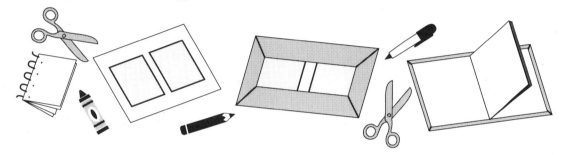

Making journals is an important part of building student ownership for journal writing. Your students can make their own journals using any of the materials listed here. Either staple pages and covers, or punch holes and use metal rings or yarn to keep pages and covers together. Encourage students to decorate and personalize the covers of both purchased and handmade journals with colored pens, stickers, and so on. This helps make the journals their very own.

Materials

pencils and pens (all kinds and colors)
crayons
date stamp and ink pad (for young children)
paper (preferably lined for older students)
tagboard or matboard
light cardboard such as cereal boxes
contact paper
wallpaper book (sample pages make durable covers)
brown paper grocery bags
construction paper
metal rings
yarn
hole punch
stapler
stickers or other stick-on letters
plastic spiral binding machine
spiral-bound notebook
looseleaf binder
plastic recloseable bags (for carrying journals to and from home)

The size of the journals students make is important. Younger children may need larger journals because they enjoy drawing pictures. Younger children also have less control over their writing and may need more space to write.

The kind of paper you use, lined or unlined, is also important. For young children, unlined paper makes sense at first, but as they begin writing, paper that is part lined and part unlined allows them to draw and write on lines, too. For older students, if legibility is a goal or a problem, lined paper tends to help.

Directions for making a bound journal follow. If you want students' journals to have lined pages, draw lines on one sheet of paper and make copies to use as journal pages. If you use unlined paper, you might give each student a heavily black-lined sheet of paper to place under the journal page. The lines will show through and can be used as a guide.

Bookbinding

Materials:

8½" × 11" paper or larger

carpet needle and thread or sewing machine

contact paper, lightweight cloth, or wallpaper

oaktag or cardboard (cereal box)

scissors

gluestick

ruler

Procedure:

1. Decide number of pages you need and fold paper in half to form 5½-inch by 4¼-inch pages (or larger).

2. Sew along the fold with a needle and heavy thread or use longest stitch on sewing machine.

3. Cut contact paper, cloth, or wall paper to about 10 inches by 13 inches to make your book's cover.

4. Cut two pieces of oaktag or cardboard that are a bit larger than the 5½-inch by 4¼-inch pages.

5. Lay the cover flat with the wrong side up. Put the oaktag or cardboard on it, leaving space between these pieces so the book can open and close easily.

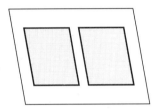

6. First, fold in the corners and glue flat. Then, fold in top, bottom, and sides, and glue to cardboard or oaktag. (This sequence makes neat corners.)

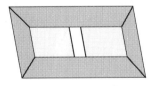

7. Glue the first page of the book to the front cover and the last page to the back cover.

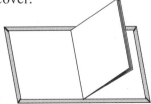

Variation: Shape Books

Cut book pages and cover into a special shape.

Professional Resources

Anderson, Jim (1993). Journal Writing: The Promise and the Reality. *Journal of Reading*, **36 (4), pp. 304-309.**

This article discusses problems associated with journal writing, such as over use, ethics, goals, and grading, and includes suggestions for making journals a useful pleasure.

Calkins, Lucy McCormick & Harwayne, Shelley (1991). *Living Between the Lines.* **Portsmouth, NH: Heinemann.**

About nurturing student learning through the reading-writing workshop, this book contains chapters worth reading on the writer's notebook as rehearsal for writing and on helping students move from notebooks to projects.

Dahlstrom, L. M. (1990). *Writing Down the Days: 365 Creative Journaling Ideas for Young People.* **Minneapolis: Free Spirit Press.**

This is a collection of serious and silly journaling ideas, one for every day of the year. Each includes a fact-filled introduction and many contain addresses that lead the way to more information. Famous people, historic events, birthdays, hobbies, hot dogs, National Goof-Off Day, popcorn, and the Peace Corps are a few of the topics included.

Fulwiler, Toby. (Ed.) (1987). *The Journal Book.* **Portsmouth, NH: Heinemann.**

This is a book written by teachers and researchers who have found journals to be a vehicle for building the language of speculation, exploring the arts and humanities, teaching English, and learning in the quantitative disciplines.

Harwayne, Shelley (1992). *Lasting Impressions: Weaving Literature into the Writing Workshop*. Portsmouth, NH: Heinemann.

The many ways that literature informs writers and the writing workshop are the focus of this book which contains an important chapter on literature and the writer's notebook.

Parsons, Les. (1990). *Response Journals*. Portsmouth, NH: Heinemann.

This handbook provides helpful ideas for responding to journals, literature, and media, guidelines for developing small group discussion, and specific ideas and instruments for evaluation by students and teachers.

Senn, J. A. (1992). *325 Creative Prompts For Personal Journals*. New York: Scholastic.

Full of thought-provoking, mind-tickling "sparks" for teachers at all grade levels to launch students into the habit of daily, meaningful, authentic writing on a range of themes as varied as fads, fables, and friendship.

Sullivan, Anne M. (1989). Liberating the Urge to Write: From Classroom Journals to Lifelong Writing. *English Journal*, 79 (7), pp. 55-60.

This article offers a set of strategies for implementing and evaluating journal writing. Sullivan shows how journal writing offers opportunities to translate experiences into language and how it satisfies a basic human need for self-expression and exploration.

Tchudi, S. & Tchudi, S. (1984). *The Young Writer's Handbook*. New York: Aladdin.

This book is "a practical guide for the beginner who is serious about writing." It presents helpful procedures and approaches for writing journals, letters, notes, stories, poems, school reports, and experiments. The author's advice and suggestions about all aspects of the writing process, including editing and publishing, are interspersed with that of well-known writers.

Weiss, H. (1974). *How To Make Your Own Books*. New York: HarperCollins.

This book has basic instructions for making a book, as well as suggestions for other bookmaking projects, including travel journals, diaries, and scrapbooks.

Wollman-Bonilla, Julie. (1991). *Response Journals: Inviting Students to Think and Write About Literature*. New York: Scholastic.

For teachers who are new to response journals and wonder why and how to get started and for those who already use them, this book gives practical ideas and solutions to common problems.